# Bible Interpretations

### Thirteenth Series
### July 1-September 30, 1894

*Matthew, Luke, John, Daniel*

# Bible Interpretations

## Thirteenth Series

*Matthew, Luke, John, Daniel*

These Bible Interpretations were published in the Inter-Ocean Newspaper in Chicago, Illinois during the late eighteen nineties.

## By
## Emma Curtis Hopkins

*President of the Emma Curtis Hopkins Theological Seminary at Chicago, Illinois*

WISEWOMAN PRESS

*Bible Interpretations: Thirteenth Series*

By Emma Curtis Hopkins

© WiseWoman Press 2012

Managing Editor: Michael Terranova

ISBN: 978-0945385-63-9

WiseWoman Press

Vancouver, WA  98665

www.wisewomanpress.com

www.emmacurtishopkins.com

# CONTENTS

|  |  |  |
|---|---|---|
|  | Foreword by Rev. Natalie R. Jean | ix |
|  | Introduction by Rev. Michael Terranova | xi |
| I. | The Birth Of Jesus | 1 |
|  | *Luke 2:1-16* |  |
| II. | Presentation In The Temple | 7 |
|  | *Luke 2:25-38* |  |
| III. | Visit Of The Wise | 15 |
|  | *Matthew 2:1-12* |  |
| IV. | Flight Into Egypt | 23 |
|  | *Matthew 2:13-23* |  |
| V. | The Youth Of Jesus | 31 |
|  | *Luke 2:40-52* |  |
| VI. | The "All Is God" Doctrine | 41 |
|  | *Mark 1: 1-11* |  |
| VII. | Missing | 49 |
| VIII. | First Disciples Of Jesus | 51 |
|  | *John 1:36-49* |  |
| IX. | The First Miracle Of Jesus | 57 |
|  | *John 2:1-11* |  |
| X. | Jesus Cleansing the Temple | 65 |
|  | *John 2:13-25* |  |
| XI. | Jesus and Nicodemus | 73 |
|  | *John 3:1-16* |  |
| XII. | Jesus at Jacobs Well | 79 |
|  | *John 4:9-26* |  |
| XIII. | Daniel's Abstinence | 87 |
|  | *Daniel 1:8-20* |  |
| XIV. | REVIEW | 95 |
|  | *John 2:13-25* |  |
|  | List of Bible Interpretation Series | 108 |

# Editors Note

All lessons starting with the Seventh Series of Bible Interpretations will be Sunday postings from the Inter-Ocean Newspaper in Chicago, Illinois. Many of the lessons in the following series were retrieved from the International New Thought Association Archives, in Mesa, Arizona by, Rev Joanna Rogers. Many others were retrieved from libraries in Chicago, and the Library of Congress, by Rev. Natalie Jean.

All the lessons follow the Sunday School Lesson Plan published in "Peloubet's International Sunday School Lessons". The passages to be studied are selected by an International Committee of traditional Bible Scholars.

Some of the Emma's lessons don't have a title. In these cases the heading will say "Comments and Explanations of the Golden Text," followed by the Bible passages to be studied.

# Foreword

*By Rev. Natalie R. Jean*

I have read many teachings by Emma Curtis Hopkins, but the teachings that touch the very essence of my soul are her Bible Interpretations. There are many books written on the teachings of the Bible, but none can touch the surface of the true messages more than these Bible interpretations. With each word you can feel and see how Spirit spoke through Emma. The mystical interpretations take you on a wonderful journey to Self Realization.

Each passage opens your consciousness to a new awareness of the realities of life. The illusions of life seem to disappear through each interpretation. Emma teaches that we are the key that unlocks the doorway to the light that shines within. She incorporates ideals of other religions into her teachings, in order to understand the commonalities, so that there is a complete understanding of our Oneness. Emma opens our eyes and mind to a better today and exciting future.

Emma Curtis Hopkins, one of the Founders of New Thought teaches us to love ourselves, to speak our Truth, and to focus on our Good. My life has moved in wonderful directions because of her teachings. I know the only thing that can move me in this world is God. May these interpretations guide you to a similar path and may you truly remember that "There Is Good For You and You Ought to Have It."

# Introduction

Emma Curtis Hopkins was born in 1849 in Killingsly, Connecticut. She passed on April 8, 1925. Mrs. Hopkins had a marvelous education and could read many of the worlds classical texts in their original language. During her extensive studies she was always able to discover the Universal Truths in each of the world's sacred traditions. She quotes from many of these teachings in her writings. As she was a very private person, we know little about her personal life. What we do know has been gleaned from other people or from the archived writings we have been able to discover.

Emma Curtis Hopkins was one of the greatest influences on the New Thought movement in the United States. She taught over 50,000 people the Universal Truth of knowing "God is All there is." She taught many of founders of early New Thought, and in turn these individuals expanded the influence of her teachings. All of her writings encourage the student to enter into a personal relationship with God. She presses us to deny anything except the Truth of this spiritual Presence in every area of our lives. This is the central focus of all her teachings.

The first six series of Bible Interpretations were presented at her seminary in Chicago, Illinois. The remaining Series', probably close to thirty, were printed in the Inter Ocean Newspaper in Chicago. Many of the lessons are no longer available for various reasons. It is the intention of WiseWoman Press to publish as many of these Bible Interpretations as possible. Our hope is that any missing lessons will be found or directed to us.

I am very honored to join the long line of people that have been involved in publishing Emma Curtis Hopkins's Bible Interpretations. Some confusion exists as to the numbering sequence of the lessons. In the early 1920's many of the lessons were published by the Highwatch Fellowship. Inadvertently the first two lessons were omitted from the numbering system. Rev. Joanna Rogers has corrected this mistake by finding the first two lessons and restoring them to their rightful place in the order. Rev. Rogers has been able to find many of the missing lessons at the International New Thought Alliance archives in Mesa, Arizona. Rev. Rogers painstakingly scoured the archives for the missing lessons as well as for Mrs. Hopkins other works. She has published much of what was discovered. WiseWoman Press is now publishing the correctly numbered series of the Bible Interpretations.

In the early 1940's, there was a resurgence of interest in Emma's works. At that time, Highwatch Fellowship began to publish many of her writings, and it was then that *High Mysticism*, her seminal work was published. Previously, the material contained in High Mysticism was only available as individual lessons and was brought together in book form for the first time. Although there were many errors in these first publications and many Bible verses were incorrectly quoted, I am happy to announce that WiseWoman Press is now publishing *High Mysticism* in the a corrected format. This corrected form was scanned faithfully from the original, individual lessons.

The next person to publish some of the Bible Lessons was Rev. Marge Flotron from the Ministry of Truth International in Chicago, Illinois. She published the Bible Lessons as well as many of Emma's other works. By her initiative, Emma's writings were brought to a larger audience when DeVorss & Company, a longtime publisher of Truth Teachings, took on the publication of her key works.

In addition, Dr. Carmelita Trowbridge, founding minister of The Sanctuary of Truth in Alhambra, California, inspired her assistant minister, Rev. Shirley Lawrence, to publish many of Emma's works, including the first three series of Bible Interpretations. Rev. Lawrence created mail order courses for many of these Series. She has graciously passed on any information she had, in order to assure that these works continue to inspire individuals and groups who are called to further study of the teachings of Mrs. Hopkins.

Finally, a very special acknowledgement goes to Rev Natalie Jean, who has worked diligently to retrieve several of Emma's lessons from the Library of Congress, as well as libraries in Chicago. Rev. Jean hand-typed many of the lessons she found on microfilm. Much of what she found is on her website, www.highwatch.net.

It is with a grateful heart that I am able to pass on these wonderful teachings. I have been studying dear Emma's works for fifteen years. I was introduced to her writings by my mentor and teacher, Rev. Marcia Sutton. I have been overjoyed with the results of delving deeply into these Truth Teachings.

In 2004, I wrote a Sacred Covenant entitled "Resurrecting Emma," and created a website, www.emmacurtishopkins.com. The result of creating this covenant and website has brought many of Emma's works into my hands and has deepened my faith in God. As a result of my love for these works, I was led to become a member of Wise-Woman Press and to publish these wonderful teachings. God is Good.

My understanding of Truth from these divinely inspired teachings keeps bringing great Joy, Freedom, and Peace to my life.

Dear reader; It is with an open heart that I offer these works to you, and I know they will touch you as they have touched me. Together we are living in the Truth that God is truly present, and living for and through each of us.

The greatest Truth Emma presented to us is "My Good is my God, Omnipresent, Omnipotent and Omniscient."

Rev. Michael Terranova

WiseWoman Press

Vancouver, Washington, 2010

# LESSON I

## The Birth Of Jesus

*Luke 2:1-16*

Pythagoras went from temple to temple in Egypt trying to learn certain mysteries which could only be learned by holding steadfast to his own mystic center of being.

His scholasticism interfered with his poise, distracting him by its habit of dissecting, vivisecting, analyzing, classifying, comparing even his most spiritual stepping stones toward the radiating center.

All philosophers, religionists, merchantmen, and seamen are struggling to get back to their mystic center of being by the daily exercise of their calling. "Whatever you yourself are this moment doing, it is your unconscious effort to find that poised point of your being from which you may consciously radiate your native wisdom, power, reality.

Jesus Christ said that nobody would instantly touch this poise except those who remembered exactly how it had been with them when they were formerly there. "No man ascendeth up into heaven save he that came down from heaven." "I came from God." According to him it is an interference with your instant poise to affirm that you are a reincarnation or a transmigrant. Since you truly did hail from that bright home, your mystic center, why dally among theories of prowling round upon an earth whose inhabitants insist that you are a detriment to their chances?

## No Room for Jesus

This lesson of Luke 2, tells us that there was no room for Jesus in the inn at Bethlehem. And there never will be. You might as well get you to your home.

For you are all one Jesus and if you insist that you hail from paradise and not from dust you can prove it. If you insist that you want to be dust with the rest of them the inn of dust will never be large enough to hold you. They will write books on "overpopulation," and tomahawk you for your wampum, or your green-backs, or your philosophy. They will make you work for a cent a month over your expense for calico and butterine (oleomargarine), or boycott you for getting their one cent away from them. You had better insist that you came forth from God, that you never lose sight of your home, and that it is now time for you to return.

Pythagoras never really touched his poised mystic center, but came near enough thereto so that he worked miracles. Jesus touched it and held himself there, thereby making himself the central figure of a planet's history. He loses the earth robes when watched as God. And it is as God he chooses to be watched, and by this everlasting and changeless choice telling all men to proclaim as one man that he and they are one.

When mankind have this truth preached to them Jesus Christ has come. Whosoever welcomes it is wise. As Pythagoras was too scholastic, so also the Sanhedrin did not see that the signals flying from battlement and tower of star and prophecy had written on their sheeny folds, "Joy to the world."

But some common laboring men, busy with their daily duties, recognized that, though invisible to them, something had taken place upon the planet. And they said: *"Let us go now even unto the place of bread and see this thing which is come to pass. And they found."* (Verses 15, 16)

## Man's Mystic Center

They did not analyze and classify the child that found no room in the inn. They did not vivisect and dissect his being. They rejoiced. They praised. They joined with Joseph and Mary in nourishing him.

The mystic center of man's being takes up no room in his flesh mind. But man struggles and strives with his flesh mind to find it there. The mere proclamation that there is such a center is all that there is to it. All who proclaim the fact arouse their secret faculties to fasten their inward gaze toward what is upon the earth but not of it.

Whoever is aware that his only business has hitherto been for the unconscious purpose of finding that center which Pythagoras was seeking instantly glorifies his every action with knowledge of why he performs it.

Did the committee on Sunday School lessons realize when they were teaching millions of people that plague, famine, pestilence, death, affliction, and so on, which they called stepping stones of man's memory, were their self-elected way of returning to their bright home whence they came out, their poised point in their being which taketh up no room in the inn of death, plague, or famine?

### They Glorify Their Performances

Does the merchantman realize when he clutches his crispy millions that they are his self-elected stepping blocks toward the mystic center whence he came out that taketh up no room in the inn of money?

Does the occultist, breathing his seven deep breaths of Prana, and his seven times seven deep breaths, realize that they are his self-elected march toward his happy poising point that taketh up no room in the inn of his breaths or their courtyards?

The moment these people do realize that all performances are for that one purpose only they glorify their performances by forgetting them. Like the shepherds on Palestine hillsides, they take a shorter way, an easier way, than afflictions, labor, and competitions.

Whoever recognizes that there is indeed such a mystic center rouses his unused visions and faculties, and rejoices that there is. Whoever must have evidence before he believes in it does not rouse his being to find it.

One is a shepherd of sheep, as parabled by Luke. The other is Pythagoras, as historied by mystics. How gentle and peaceable is the one who saith, *"I came forth from God. I dwell in God. I return to God."* How majestic his character! How universal his reign! He ruleth the spheres with a rod of unbreakable iron. None can withstand him. He is not looking to the ways of the flesh. He feeleth not the cold, the blows of being unrecognized, unhoused by the world of dust. *"My kingdom is an everlasting kingdom — not of this world, yet with you always."*

*Inter-Ocean Newspaper   July 1, 1894*

# LESSON II

# Presentation In The Temple

*Luke 2:25-38*

There is a spiritual sun that lights the intelligence of man as there is a physical sun to light the growth of trees. Whoever understands how to place his own intelligence under the rays of the spiritual sun acts the part of the wise gardener setting his plants in happy exposures. Many miracles have been wrought by unwittingly setting the mind into the spiritual sunshine. Lately a woman wrote to a wise little journal an account of how she wrought a miracle as wonderful as the increasing of the loaves and fishes. She was in debt, and took her case to the Lord, whose bright presence fills heaven and earth, who answers prayers, who defends, protects, provides for his people.

She took a non-anxious attitude of mind, and waited for the spirit that it has been promised should teach all things, that Son of Man's wisdom to lighten his speech and actions, to come and inform her what to do. It came while she waited, sitting alone far into the night's still hours, as an interior shining. She asked what she should do, and then the wonderful miracle took place.

If the thousands upon thousands of penniless men and women in our country would do likewise, they would not need to take any other measures whatsoever to protect themselves from the subtle movements of darkness now attempting to make Russian serfs of them.

## A Light for Every Man

For there is a light to lighten every man that cometh into the world. And that light is the life of men, the support and wisdom, of men, the absolute freedom of men from the clutches of environment. Each man has it. It is not in the power of the rich, to withhold it from the poor, nor of the poor to withhold it from the rich. It makes no distinction as to race, color, sex, or education. It is the impartial sunshine of an all-giving spiritual light that can unto all these convey independent supply.

He who shall first burst upon the world with unfailing signals of his understanding of the spiritual sunshine will strike the shackles off mankind in the lightning flash of one lesson, and "let my people go."

Not to the anxious-hearted, but to the watchers of the light. "Martha, Martha, thou art troubled, but Mary watcheth the light." The gardener who understands the sunshine is not anxious; he knows what miraculous energies move through loam and leaf at the first fall of heat from the faithful sunlight.

The sunshine rolls the thunders and discharges the volcanoes. The sunshine moves the ocean's resistless tides and tints the violet's face. Fires and avalanches, dust and muscle smile with successful fulfillments when they are acquainted with the sun.

Therefore the light of the mind, the sunshine of the soul, saith unto all men everywhere: "Acquaint now thyself with me and be at peace."

And it saith: "Be not anxious but watch for the light." And it saith: "Fret not thyself because of evil doers, but watch for the light."

## All Things are Revealed

The spiritual sun is the true light. It is the light that lighteth every man, and if he seeth it "no evil ever cometh nigh his dwelling." All things are revealed unto him. Wheresoever the spirit moveth there he is found, as today's Bible lesson reads of Simeon.

When the spirit goeth swiftly, man being glorified by it, maketh haste, as Jesus driving into the wilderness, one with the light to set his intelligence under its full shining so that he might settle the question of which ego of man is the victorious man.

Paracelsus, making a study of all the egos, namely, the senses' "I am," which says, "I am in pain, I am too hot, or too cold;" the intellect's "I am" which says, "I am highly intelligent, or I am entirely stupid;" the human soul's "I am," which says, "I am restless, or I am at peace," wrote: "There are some persons who live in this interior light, but the life of others is centered in their animal instincts. Those who live in their animal instincts are inspired by their animal reason, and if they write it is dictated by the animal reason. Some write from the intellectual reason; some from the spiritual light. A person who writes should know the cause from which his ideas come."

And the time has now come when all men should know which reasoner, or ego, they are managing their life by.

If a man speaks or writes from the light of policy he will handle the question by the lamp of his human ego. He will argue bravely on the side of his pocket-book's interest and browbeat his unscheming neighbor's truth.

But that light is darkness, and Jesus Christ the truth, though a little child just spoken is set for the fall of all such as reason by human policy, intellectual computation, or the animal instincts. This is the meaning of Simeon's prophecy. (Luke 2:34)

## The Coming Power

Simeon had been watching the true light that shineth for all in the world, to be boldly preached and practiced by some one man. When Joseph and Mary brought the young child into the temple the spiritual intimation of the coming power and splendor of the doctrine that boy would preach came over Simeon, and he chanted the wonderful *Nunc dimittis*, "Lord, now thou art letting me depart in peace."

Each age repeats the story of truth being spoken by somebody who gets brow-beaten and snubbed for his first utterance thereof because he speaks so newly to the world.

This is the little boy in the temple, too poor to pay the government's money taxes, just slipping in by a pair of turtle doves, but destined to overthrow the government, destroy the temple and make his living entirely independent of the financial policies of the age into which he cometh, learn his lessons entirely independent of the world's school systems, inform mankind of the folly and nonsense of studying *"mastodon giganteus,"* or the animal ego, asteroids, and art, or the intellect's ego, for the Holy Spirit is a perfect teacher, a perfect provider, "the glory of thy people Israel."

It may put millions into a man's pockets to watch the animal wants of men and cater to them. It may put fame into a man's pockets to watch the intellectual wants of men and cater to them with conic sections and mythology, but it is not the light of God shining on their intelligence to do it. It is not Jesus Christ. He teaches that by the sunshine of the Holy Spirit all the native wants of men are supplied and then disappear.

First, the miracle of food and payments of all obligations without human assistance, then nevermore to need food or money.

First, the knowledge of all things in heaven above or earth beneath without human instruction, and then nevermore to deal with such informations.

## Like the Noonday Sun

For the spirit needeth not that any man should teach it; the spirit needeth not that any man should feed it. The spirit, shining straight on the intelligence of man, shineth down and out all other egos, as shadows are sunned away at noon time. The young child is now in the world. Only the spiritually inclined see him. It is the young doctrine being brought forward by these lessons. It stirs men over the planet to ask for light on the question of why it happens, if all men are born free and equal, that a few of them have such multitudes by the neck.

They are told that by putting their intelligence under the sunlight of this young truth they become entirely independent of other men's assistance toward providing for their material bodies or instructing their intellects.

*"For the flesh profiteth nothing" and "the natural mind receiveth not the things of the spirit, for they are foolishness unto him, but the spiritual man judgeth of all things, and is himself judged of no man."*

Under the sunny truth of the spirit the intelligence of all men, in all climes and times, is able to prove that it is one free, independent life, one free, independent substance.

The doctrine that man is spirit only, the flesh profiteth nothing, is as the child in the temple of the religious teachings of a planet.

Whoever recognizes that it is the doctrine that shall cause the material earth to melt away as a mist and the elements to disappear, for the spiritual earth and its inhabitants to appear and to abide, acts as the prophet to his age.

All is the unreality of a shadow that declineth except the spirit in man. That is the sacred plant that is shone upon by the everlasting God that fainteth not.

The body of matter fainteth for lack of nourishment. The intellect declineth for lack of restoring, but the spirit of man shineth more and more unto the perfect day.

Whosoever fainteth for lack of reviving help, let him set his intelligence in the sunshine of the Jesus Christ declaration. *"I and the Father are one."*

*Inter-Ocean Newspaper July 8, 1894*

# LESSON III

# Visit Of The Wise

*Matthew 2:1-12*

### Twelve Principles in the Mind of Man Nations Should Acknowledge God as Our Father

There are twelve undemolishable principles already laid in the mind of man. As soon as one of these principles is uncovered by preaching it, there grows out a warfare between .the people who see the principle and those who are determined not to see it.

*"I came not to bring peace but a sword."*

Never take into consideration how much it will cost you in dollars and cents if you espouse the principle when it is uncovered. Never take notice of how much inconvenience it will be to yourself or to anybody else if you advocate the principle latest exposed.

Of any institution founded on the right of material advantage over human right it is promised that *"there shall not be one stone upon another that shall not be torn down."*

Of any city founded on the material advantage of a single body over the human right of one or many it is written, and nothing can stop the fulfillment thereof, "Behold your house is left unto you desolate."

To stop to consider material losses or gains is small business while an eternal principle is managing the situation. The principle will win. If a nation has had so awful a principle as that all men are created free and equal exposed as a stone plank in its platform, what can that nation expect but the tearing down of any institution within its borders that disputes it?

## The Law Our Teacher

A good school-teacher overturns first one state of affairs and then another in a school-room, where other teachers have let them reign. Paul says that "the law is our schoolmaster." The way a principle acts when it is exposed is something terrible.

Take a nation with that principle of God having been the common Father of all men, and see how first one yoke and then another gets slipped off the people belonging to it. They do not need any firearms on their side. They do not need the alliance of rich men. They do not need to be learned. Staying at home or walking the streets, befriended or friendless, it's all one. The almighty principle is equal to anything.

> *"Thrice is he arm'd that hath his quarrel just;*
>
> *And he but naked, though lock'd up in steel,*
>
> *Whose conscience with injustice is corrupted."*

Take notice of the principle itself, whatever the principle is, that is up last for a world's consideration. Once in about so long mankind has to face a principle. It stands out so terribly determined to be looked at that none can take his mind's eye off it. Have you money to offer the principle? No? Well, it does not need money. It never asked for anything whatsoever except your gaze of mind. *"Look unto me and be ye saved." "Stand thou still, and see what the Lord shall do for thee this day."*

> *"Say, shall we yield him in costly devotion*
>
> *Odors of Edom and offerings divine?*
>
> *Gems of the mountains and pearls of the ocean,*
>
> *Myrrh from the forest, and gold from the mine?*
>
> *Vainly we offer each ample oblation,*
>
> *Vainly with gifts would his favor secure.*

*Richer by far is the heart's adoration;*

*Dearer to God are the prayers of the poor."*

## Take neither Scrip nor Purse

Every principle exposed is a smile on the face of God. Jesus Christ said whoever should see it need salute no man by the way and need not take cither purse or scrip for his journey. That is, need not think of so material matters as money or inconveniences.

If a man's purse has little in it he feels the burden of it worse than if it is full. But if he has his eye on the last principle of righteousness, exposed by much talking up, he may ignore the subject of purses and yet have enough to eat, drink, and wear.

If he is troubled about anything he has a scrip or writing on his heart that weights him down. Mary Tudor said if they should uncover her heart they would find written across it "Calais." Lo, every heart knoweth its own bitterness or scrip. But while you are watching a principle, ignore the scrip, or your grievance.

*"I am the Lord that healeth thee.*

*As one whom his mother comforteth*

*So will I comfort thee."*

When one of the twelve principles is uncovered to the extent that the ruling state of affairs in a realm gets intimation that its reign must be overthrown it is then at exactly the state of things taught by this lesson of (Matt, 2:1-12.)

Herod, with all his hierarchy, "was troubled" because the principle of equal birth from one common father was already come into his nation, and he could see that the practice of tyranny must be dissolved by it.

"Herod" represents the king of whatever nation uncovers the eternal principle of the equal origin of man. Today the lesson on the "wise men," "Joseph and Mary," "Herod and the scribes," takes in the state of the whole world. For the end of regarding scripture parables as referring to one nation only has come.

## The Star in the East

One Herod now is king of the fourth globe of our constellation. You will find the end of that Herod prophesied in Revelations 18.

The "star in the east" is that religious teaching which assures and reassures mankind that it is an unquestionable certainty that the principle now up for investigation is the triumphing Jesus Christ.

Only the magi of the world are confident of its absoluteness success. The magi are the "wise men". (Verse 1) They came from the Orient. All the intuitive faculties are cultivated to the highest extent in the Oriental districts of our globe, and, gradually fascinating the Occident, find their live demonstration there.

*"Westward the course of empire takes its way,*

   *The first four acts already past;*

*The fifth shall close the drama with a day.*

   *Time's noblest offspring be the last."*

The magi of old were those among the Persians and Medes who cultivated occult science. Herodotus tells of them as representing all that was best in ancient learning. Daniel was president of the order of the magi in Babylon. They found out everything by intuitive readings. They journeyed westward to Bethlehem and gave their testimonies, the arrival of the undemolishable teachings that had been promised for generations for the overthrow of material tyranny.

They explained that what was then transpired for Judea was to transpire in a latter age for a whole globe (Verse 6), when not one man, but the agreement of many men, should represent Herod, and a leveling principle should by its own quality, utterly dissolve their agreement. (Rev. 18)

## The Influence of Truth

There is something inspiring to praise and worship in the knowledge of these twelve irresistible truths, or principles, or axioms, implanted in every mind alike. When we suddenly come upon one of them we fall like the magi before it. When we realize them all in one setting, and can see with unhindered vision that they shall reign from zone to zone, we then know what the magi of old knew was meant by the one name — Jesus Christ.

Mind is one. The twelve eternal truths of mind are as solidly laid in the ditch digger's mind as in the mind of our President. The instant he uncovers one of these awful principles, and knows its meaning, he becomes an irresistible foe to handle.

The colored mothers of the South had no money, no firearms, no learning of the schools, but on their bended knees they discovered that "one God hath made us, of one blood all the nations," and in rapt adoration they kissed the smile of that truth.

*"Put golden padlocks on Truth's lips,*

    *be callous as ye will,*

*From soul to soul o'er all the world*

    *leaps one electric thrill."*

*Inter-Ocean Newspaper July 15, 1894*

# LESSON IV

# Flight Into Egypt

*Matthew 2:13-23*

**Principle That Is Represented By Jesus Of Nazareth**

**Cry of the Wage Earner Outward Signal Of The Presence Of The King Of Kings And Lord Of Lords**

Apocryphal legends serve the truth that the journey of those who nourished the coming conqueror was miraculously shortened when they fled into defeated exile.

The story of those people who see any truth and cherish it is explained by the story of Joseph and Mary. The effect of that one truth when it is recognized by a few esoteric minds is told by the actions of Herod of Judea and his counselors and soldiers.

The particular principle Jesus of Nazareth represented was universal freedom. No man or set of men should have any other man or set of men by the throat in any literal or figurative fashion. By his presence it should be made absolutely impossible for any combination of "brainy men" to gather the atmospheres of the world into their own storehouses, put meters into other men's necks and charge them a penny a week or so for breath.

Neither should there arise a combination that should collect the coal products of the universally impartial earth and charge a penny an hour or so for warmth. The very first sign of the grown-up presence of the living Jesus Christ among men must be the "share and share alike" practice. Those who were actually in understanding of the doctrine of Jesus "shared all things in common," as we read in history. (Acts 2:44)

By his presence the painter of the Madonna's countenance, though that face smile down with entrancing radiance, should not receive one mite of wages more per day for his labor than should the typesetter in a printing office. The question should not be "What job were you at and how much did you accomplish at it?" but "Did you do the best you could under the circumstances?"

## The Magic Word of Wage Earning

The magic word of wage earning should be, "The best I could." The owner of the shops should not have one penny more per day for doing the best he could than should the girl who mopped the marble pavement leading to the shops. This does not claim to be civilization as taught by Harvard University, but it is Jesus Christ as now come into this closing era through the awfully silent, but omnipotently intentioned second coming of Jesus.

What its ministry tells in secret the masses yell upon the housetops and Herod with his battalions object to openly. (Matt. 10: 27)

It is the lion of the tribe of Judah who when he first roars his intentions is so young that he is easily hustled back into his cage again, but at each period of his roaring he is less manageable and finally at one glance of his almighty eyes the Herodian-Roman battalions fall prostrate on their faces. At one lift of a little whip of thongs glistening with the light of this heaven-descended principle the manipulators of stocks and bonds skip the planet. (Matt. 21:12)

It is not written of him that he hurt the soldiers, but they could not touch him. It is not written that the money-holders were hurt by the whip, but the sight of it over-threw their counters and scattered the contents of their banks.

By the mystic energies of Christian principles when they are printed on paper or metal or cloth by the enlightened thoughts of a few, the very money handled in banks and stores becomes a whip of thongs; becomes dynamite. Was it not written that the aprons and handkerchiefs of Paul healed the sick? Shall it not be that the paper and metal used by the Christians who know the mind of Jesus concerning the true wage-earning principle shall cure the poverty of the masses?

## How Knowledge Affects the Times

This principle of universal freedom whose effect is every man getting equal share with every other man on the heaven-conceived idea of doing their best has seven stages of effect on the outside world when it is secretly known to a few magi.

1. The masses begin to discover that they are getting tightened, and wonder what the cause is. They get to striking their arms around like the little hungry baby in the manger at Bethlehem.

2. The masses, who are first to feel the stir of the Jesus Christ ministry as it is preached in secret, get into disfavor with the powers of civilization, like the little 6 weeks old child of Matt 2:1-12.

3. The masses are hurried back into obscurity again as Jesus was hurried into Egypt — (Matt. 2.)

4. The masses begin to instruct the pulpits as to what constitutes Jesus Christ principles, as the 12 years old Jesus taught the learned rabbis. *Vox-populi, vox Dei*. Christ is the truth. He who feels and speaks truth is Jesus.

5. The voice of God is plainly heard by man independent of the schools and governments of earth — Mark 1:11.

6. Prosperity by spiritual inspiration and prosperity by civilization's methods are the option of the masses. They choose spiritual inspiration — Matt. 4:11.

7. The new education of church and school adopts the principle of equal wages for each man's best — John 1:49.

As this heaven-born principle is now operating from its mystic center through the voice of the masses we as a world under its young announcements are pictured by today's international religious propositions. Those who feel, but cannot speak what the real intentions of the texts amount to, are the people who are working in shops and on farms, in ditches and on newspapers. The secret doctrine is stirring them openly. The secret doctrine is that if a man does the best he can he has a right to exactly the same wages as his neighbor man who does the best he can, irrespective of what he is working at, whether flourishing his rhetoric in a pulpit or polishing Vanderbilt's boots.

## The Awakening of the Common People

This is the unworded feeling that is stirring the breasts of what are called "common people." It is forever recorded that "the common people heard this Jesus Christ doctrine gladly," but the rich men and the mighty men, the governors and princes, the fashionable and the daintily clad, howled with disfavor. (Mark 12)

Today's lesson represents the people who feel the inward stir of this heaven-arrived truth as being driven back into their cages again under the figure of the little Jesus being carried down into Egypt. (Matt. 2) But, remember, the lion of the tribe of Judah is an unkillable beast. On his brow is stamped in letters of light, "Conquering and to Conquer."

The newspapers record these things as strikes and fights. But in the workshop of Jehovah, where Jesus Christ's principles are born, they are known as the outward signals of the young King of Kings and Lord of Lords in our midst. And that king is only a true principle practiced in heaven arrived on our earth in answer to the earnest prayers of our mothers:

"Thy kingdom come, thy will be done, on earth as it is in heaven."

Who is hoping to defeat that offspring of Jehovah, the eternal principle and practice in heaven, viz: Wages for doing the best you could under the circumstances — man at eleventh hour equal to man at third hour, because he did the best his opportunity admitted? (Matt. 20)

*"Heart's truth is quick witted;*

　*The schools are sad and slow;*

*The masters quite omitted*

　*The lore we care to know."*

*Inter-Ocean Newspaper July 22, 1894*

# LESSON V

## The Youth Of Jesus

*Luke 2:40-52*

Looking straight into thine eyes, from every infinitesimal point in space, and through every object, is the "I AM." It is the starting point of everything. Whoever recognizes it finds himself doing unusual and commonplace things with wonderful spirit and life. The language he uses may be with some difficulty, as it were, wrung from him, so that he even appears, superficially observed, to be at a disadvantage with his gifted neighbors. But every sentence is vascula; it is not astral shell, it bleeds with red life at whatever point you lance it.

Whoever has faced the "I AM," whether its attentive gaze seemed fronting him from a far off throne in the distant skies, or pointing its eternal vision through men and rocks, has been a marked character. The young Jesus saw it. He called it "the Father." Whatever he did seemed from that "I AM" starting point, or "Father." "Did ye not know that I must be about my Father's business?" (Verse 49) Nothing interfered with it in his line of march, and nothing interfered with him while he saw it, to the time when he rolled back the walls of death and proved that to see the Father's "I AM" is unkillable life.

There either is or there is not the face of "the Father" everywhere attentive to thee. Search — for if it is, then when thou seest it, thou art not a performer by the counting-house methods of the astral-shell business world. Thou amassest not wealth at the expense of thy fellow men, but on the contrary thou art a constant resource of prosperity to them, drawn by thee from the infinite storehouse of the "I AM" that looketh at thee from every infinitesimal point of environment. "He giveth to all men liberally" through thee.

## Your Righteousness Is As Filthy Rags

If thou seest the face of "the Father", thou needst not to build a monument to thy name to ease thy conscience for the vampire delusion of running little children through the long days to carry more gold pieces to thy hollow iron boxes.

If thou seest it, thou needst not to declare that thy neighbor is an adulterer, a dishonest financier, a liar, a hypocrite, or a boasting ignoramus in order to carry thyself higher in other neighbors' estimation. No tricks of trade are needed by thee in order to live and walk in majesty, a conqueror of destiny over this planet.

If thou seest it, thou needst not fear that thou shalt fail by espousing the principle of the equal worthiness of the tramp and convict to thy comradeship with the learned and pious, for thou wilt see the "I AM" face equally present in all alike. The righteousness of the righteous shall be seen to be as much of a veil over the face of the God in man as the folly of the tramp, for "all your righteousness is as filthy rags," (Isaiah 84:6) saith the Lord, and "I will cut off both the righteous and the wicked together." (see Genesis 18:23)

To see the righteousness of the righteous is equally deluding with seeing the un-righteousness of the wicked, for the only real sight is sight of the "I AM" point that looketh at thee from every infinitesimal atom of matter and mind.

## Whatsoever Ye Search. That Will Ye Find

It is the integrity point, omnipresent, whether seen or not by us; and, when seen, we are no longer occupied with descriptions of anything but it. In whosoever face or character we detect it, we may count on the long life and prosperity of that one. It was Jesus, the Carpenter of Nazareth, who was able to see this starting or "Father" point in the anarchist and tramp as well as in the rabbi's face. It is understanding of truth that enables us to watch until we see it in every face equally.

The great Being men have imagined on some far-off throne, when steadfastly watched, discloses the integrity point; and the manna that falls from sight of it, men call answer to prayer. The close pressure of mercy and the kind way our life is managed, expose the nearness of the "I AM." Whoever sees it sees as a little child. "Their faces do always behold the face of the Father." (Matt. 18:10)

Whoever starts out to see the everlasting "I AM" in all men will find his sight thereof "growing and waxing strong." (Verse 40) Our lesson is "The Youth of Jesus," (Luke 2:40-52.) Not only is it the description of a child who never had seen anything else but the face of the Father in all men and all things, but it is our history after we accept the idea that the "I AM" is in all men equally present.

There comes a time when "the grace of God is upon us." (Verse 40) It is when we have persistently watched for God everywhere for twelve years.

"And when he was twelve years old, they went up to Jerusalem after the custom of the feast." (Verse 42)

## The Starting Point Of All Men

Spiritual science is founded on the principle or truth that the starting point of all men is one. That it never is absent from any man. That it is the only reality of any man, whether he seems to be in a prison or in a pulpit. That the steadfast watching for that ever-present reality in men will surely disclose it. If we run away from the subject of our purpose and see our neighbors as ungodly beings, we do not get to the age of twelve years in persistence of search after the divinity in man. For age, in mystic science, is reckoned by points of grace, not by years of time.

It is not necessary to watch thine enemies and work to defend thyself from them. The sight of the "I AM" anywhere by thee will dissolve thy enemies. Keep watch of it and see what mighty, mighty things it will do for thee. *"No weapon that is formed against thee shall prosper."* (Isaiah 54:17)

It is not necessary to defend thyself from the burdens of nature. "Stand still and see what wonderful things the Lord will work for thee." It is not necessary to try to love thy neighbors. Wheresoever thou art best able to see the "I AM," stay thou there much. That is prayer. That is staying at home. The child Jesus stayed at home for 30 years. That is, he stayed where he could best realize the "I AM." There is no reliable record of his diffusing himself abroad and fighting with human nature to see the God-face in the Scribes and Pharisees, or the tramps and criminals. He stopped in that place where he could best realize the God everywhere looking at him till he was so strong that no other sight could possibly distract him.

Once only he spoke, and that was to the men who were talking of the God whose face he was watching. This was at Jerusalem when he was twelve years old in mystic strength. It was the same with Moses. At one point of his career, at noting the every-where-fronting God, he made a bold attempt, which created so much criticism and grief that he again retired to silence. He had then counted more solar years than this boy, Jesus, but was arrived at the same point of mystic years, viz, twelve. *"Thy father and I have sought thee sorrowing."* (Verse 48)

Moses was full of timidity and could make no show of ability before men. But he saw the "I AM." *"Tell the people that I AM hath sent thee."* (Exodus 3:14) Nerved and fired by it, he became the most marvelous labor leader of history. He who hath lost personal ambition by sight of God will lead the down-pressed millions successfully out of poverty. He who hath lost personal acquisitiveness will show the masses how bountiful is their God, and able to provide for those that see Him, whether all the products of nature have been monopolized by the few or not.

## Equal Division: the Lesson Taught by Jesus

The bountiful God that showed how the mountains, fields, mines and rivers did, by native energies, throw forth enough and to spare for all the inhabitants of earth, is able to provide in other ways just as liberally, letting the greedy "sets" of human kind have the whole that earth hath provided.

The ethers are full of that substance out of which all things are formed. The breath of man is full of commanding that can result in clothing and food.

What formed the earth, and its rich storehouses? "By the word of the I AM were the heavens formed, and the hosts of them." May not every man be one with the Mind that is God so that his word can form whatsoever he pleaseth? *"The works that I do ye shall do also."* (John 14:12)

Seneca is sometimes praised for teaching a moral science that had no rewards in it. He is compared with Jesus, who was all the time advancing the idea of results, rewards, effects, profits, advantages. This one man spoke straight to the God-point fronting him continually, and the gracious promises that fell from his lips were a comfort and encouragement to the masses. They saw that the things their daily labor was directed to attain might be dropped as manna from the

Rock of refuge, the everlasting God. They saw Jesus walking around, hoarding up nothing, one with themselves, but able to make all things out of his mind's decrees.

They heard him say, *"Where I am there ye may be also."* They saw him give and give and give, drawing all his givings straight from the Spirit, asking nothing of them but to see the face of God looking at them from every point of creation.

But they saw the proud Seneca, boasting of a science which mentioned no liberal bounty of a God — who made no distinction between rich and poor, hoarding up his millions like a modern church saint, obtained, as history relates, by all the arts of modern monopoly. He, by the same skill that is extolled in our day, amassed $15 million while "raising altars to poverty" and, in most splendid diction, denouncing the Jesus system of rewards. They saw him telling of the beauty and gladness of clemency while joining with Nero in burning the Christians who had set out on the purpose of seeing the face of God everywhere.

## The True Heart Never Falters

It is one thing to talk of the face of God and another thing to see it. He who sees it hoards up nothing, gives all, yet lacks nothing. This is truth.

He who sees it turns his right cheek to be slapped, lets his accusers have their own way, yet his character's pure shining never dims. This is truth.

He, who sees it tells of the bounty and protection of it and gets insulted for speaking of its marvelous goodness to the children of men, yet is the true heart of mankind punctured with conviction of the power and tenderness and mercy of the everlasting Father. This is truth.

It is written of even Joseph and Mary, who had followed the science of God to this point, that here *"they understood not the saying."* (Verse 50) Who is there that now understands that the face of the Father is looking out at us from every object near and far, imagined or visible? If we do not understand it — that is, do not see the face — we must, like Jesus and Moses, stay in some place where we are not distracted from sight of it for the period of twelve years. This means that period of practice of sight of the everywhere-fronting God point, which we find necessary for fixing our vision to sight of God only till nothing that is done or said diverts us into sight of anything else.

*"He who undiverted looks toward me; I will make my abode in him."* (see John 14:23)

Thus seeing the God face everywhere, the twelve mystic mileposts of solid practice were passed by Jesus. This daily fasting of sight is here called "increase in wisdom, stature, and favor with God and man." (Verse 40)

*"Thou art my all my theme, my inspiration and my crown;*

*My soul's ambition, pleasure, wealth, my world.*

*Thou art my light in darkness and my life in death.*

*Thou art my strength in age, my rise from low estate.*

*Eternity's too short to speak thy praise*

*Or fathom thy profound, deep love to man."*

*Inter-Ocean Newspaper July 29, 1894*

# LESSON VI

# The "All Is God" Doctrine

## *Mark 1: 1-11*

### Three Designated Stages of Spiritual Science

Spiritual science has three stages: Adam, Joshua, Christ. The Adam mind names both good and evil. The Joshua or Jesus mind names good only. The Christ mind names neither good nor evil; too pure to behold iniquity, too poised to be stimulated by praise. The Adam mind is the human, carnal, mortal. The Jesus or saving mind is the mind that detects that "through evil and through good, one beneficent tendency evermore streams."

The Adam mind says that "poppy heads have stupefying energy, but nature furnishes an antidote up to a certain point." The Jesus or Joshua mind says the neutral to poppy stupor is the only reality. The stupor is unreality. The Christ mind says; "Though walking through your world of goods and evils, I am not of it." When its lessons are embodied in the life of a minister, he speaks for his hearers that "they be not taken out of the world but kept from it."

Joshua is persistently determined to see and gather grapes of Eschol, where his neighbors are afraid to breathe. The Christ mind tastes the wine and bread of a kingdom where neither moth nor rust could possibly corrupt, and thoughts of evil do not have to be faithfully eliminated. One stage of Christian science is the heroic Joshua doctrine of "all is good."

The freest doctrine that can be preached is the Christ doctrine. If the praises and favors of a single human being have power to sweeten and cheer my heart, it is not a Christ heart. If the condemnations of one or many have power to depress my heart, it is not a safe heart. The free heart is independent. Its outward radiance is read in religious lore as, *"None of these things move me."* (Acts 20:24)

The Christ free principle is mentioned by David under the figure of *"a handful of corn upon the top of the mountain, the fruit whereof shall shake like Lebanon, and they that be of the city shall flourish."* (Psalms 72:16) Corn is the rich and prospering principle. Mountain is supreme attention to mind. City is living exhibition.

## Christ Alone Gives Freedom

Even if you say that it is too ideal for practice to dwell on the mountain heights of recognition of an Indwelling Presence out of the reach of praise and blame, good and evil, you will nevertheless admit that it is a state of freedom. The Christ doctrine will as certainly lead to that freedom as you look toward it.

The apparent absence, invisibility, silence of Christ today is because of His unattached freedom from good and evil. This is purity. The Christ presence among us is so pure that we, looking into it, behold our own image, our own science, as in a pool. We might see the Christ. This is truth. It is a mountain-top doctrine. Nothing smothers it. It is not interfered with by other religions, not overshadowed by any, not like unto any of them. But whoever accepts it, throws off first one weight and then another.

*"Till he at length is free.*

*Leaving his outgrown shell*

*By life's unresting sea."*

The Christ quality is perpetually insisting that it has its everlasting abode in all men alike. It came with you when you came to this planet, it is in you now, it will go with you when you ascend without tasting the tomb, or descend tasting it. It will travel with you through the astral regions, and with you alight again on this ball of sand and flesh, if you know so little of the Christ as to reincarnate.

The least attention to it makes for throwing off existing conditions. Absolute attention to it dissolves everything. It urges nothing. It pushes nothing. It asks nothing. Your Adam habit of naming evil and good gets dissolved into naming good only, while the evil is burned as chaff if you look to the science of good or Joshua, which is the first lift of mind toward Christ.

Your Joshua heroics of standing to the good only till evil is put into absolute nothingness is dissolved into something for which there is neither name nor description when your mind's attention once springs to the Christ freedom, where "None of these things move me."

Even reading this principle over once, while yet scornful at it, is sufficient impetus for your mind to cause you one day to stand unexpectedly for some uprising of mankind, which now you condemn.

It is a "corn" that shakes off the very thoughts of the mind, even as it shakes off the habits of the carnal Adam. The child feels its "I AM" presence in him, and wonders why his parents talk is so opposed to it. The child feels it when in its still, wordless majesty it says: "This is my body breaking through you." Youth feels its wondrous presence, and if youth would never look toward the business world's dodges, never temporize with the pulpit's salary reasons, the glory of this everabiding body would certainly break through all youth as the conquering principle.

At every halting place on life's journey, from childhood to youth, youth to middle age, middle age to old age, old age to senility, the unlanguaged "I AM" says: "This is my body breaking through you." The lines on the face, the color of the hair, the spring of the step, exhibit what body received the mind's attention at the halting lines, it is Lot's wife that looks back and becomes a pillar of salted attention to the past precepts, whether of Adam or Joshua.

Moses saw that all the sons of men were free by right. He watched that truth so constantly for nearly 40 years that he supposed all men would see it when he fought for it. He threw off the Egyptian who was oppressing the Israelite, supposing the Israelites would recognize the principle of free life for bond slaves. But even the bond slaves condemned him, and he had to retire into the mountains of Sinai "to watch" the "I AM" another 40 years. It then took possession of him, and at the lift of his hand, two million down-pressed men threw down their implements of labor and struck for free use of the earth.

## The Great Leaders Of Strikes

This strike was a success because Moses had watched the free Christ for nearly 60 years. *"What I say unto you I say unto all, watch."* (Mark 13:37)

Then Jesus took up the story and for twelve years watched the free Christ. Supposing that all religious teachers would hail the freedom of mankind from matter and evil, he spoke the wondrous principle aloud, but it created so much dissension that he, like Moses, retired again to watch it for 18 years past twelve.

Then he again appeared, and at the lift of his hand, a world laid down its thoughts with which it had labored so in vain and struck for freedom from pain, death, grief. "A man's word is his only burden." *"He led captivity itself captive."*

The Jesus freedom from the oppressive commandments of religion, under which we are told to expect pain, disappointment, death, is barely spoken when the world feels the shakes of the second coming of the free Christ. *"For the elect's sake these days shall be shortened."* (Mark 13:20) So swift is the operation of the Christ as compared with the Jesus that even as we dip into the cleansing Jordan of the doctrine of "all is God, and that which is not God has no existence," the baptism from on high falls on our heads.

Whoever catches the truth of the "all is God" doctrine feels its cleansing waters, whether he enters in deeply or tampers slightly. He feels the still more marvelous influence of its higher reasonings before he is aware. It is not possible to sit on the right hand and insist that the good shall reign without looking above.

One handful of people receiving the free Christ out of the reach of honor and dishonor shakes the heavens and the earth into recognition of the white splendor that is this moment falling on the soul of all humanity.

Whatever the clash and clamor, whatever the pain and terror, the days thereof shall be short. John the Baptist, who stands for Moses, Joshua and Jesus, has hardly finished his heroic ministry called science of good, before the Christ ministry, requiring no heroism falleth on man, and beast and plant. The new time has descended. The whole world is now under the new influence as we apply the lesson to our own age. This is easily readable in the parable of Mark 1.

*Inter-Ocean Newspaper August 5, 1894*

# Lesson VII

# Missing

# LESSON VIII

# First Disciples Of Jesus

### John 1:36-49

It makes no difference how much or how little brain you have coiled up in your skull, if you know the secret of drawing on the universal intelligence you can renew, re-enforce, and rejuvenate your mind *ad infinitum*. The first step toward acquaintance with your own conduit to omniscience is Self-treatment. Talk to the divinity at the starting point of your own being. Drive past your miserable semblance of body, past your miserable semblance of mind, and strike straight into the majestic splendor of your un-manifest "I Am."

The young Jesus did that way. He was outwardly born of humble parentage, in a village held in contempt, had few opportunities, associated with simple villagers, yet, he discovered the simple exercise of addressing his Independent Absolute, and at thirty years of age burst forth as the glory of men and angels.

Recognition is not what you are after. It is the fact of yourself. "The best citizens" of Nazareth raised a mob and drove Jesus out of town. "The best citizens" exiled Dante. Aristides got too just. But these men had their mind's eye and their mind's tongue directed toward their concealed origin.

## The Meaning of Repentance

For the whole past, men are looking outward over the recognition of themselves vouchsafed by their families, neighbors, communities, nations. They slink and shrink and faint, at contempt, ridicule, backbiting; they rouse, smile, beautify, energize with honor, esteem, praise. Therefore Jesus the Self-Aroused, said. "Repent." That is, turn back; and "bring forth, therefore, the works meet for repentance." Know you not that "repenting" means looking back toward yourself instead of forward toward estimations?

There came a moment when Jesus saw what Socrates, Plato, Buddha had seen before him, viz., that every personality outside of us, upon whose friendship or enmity we have laid such stress, is only the fixed form of certain swift opinions of ourselves we once let ourselves have and then forgot them. The universe is a yielding collodion or impressible ether. It is as willing to have its present arrangements erased as to hold them. If man once holds himself as a worthy being with a tough chance, he may hold that opinion only an instant, he may go away and forget about it in his determination to beat his chance, but he will find the collodion will not forget. The sensitized plate in the photographer's room does not forget. There you are twenty years afterward with your recorded freckles or high collar.

## Erase the Instructed Mind

So Jesus saw the wisdom of erasing his instructed mind and losing himself in the Self. Buddha had said before him, "Only the Self is lord over the self," meaning; "Only thine original majesty, which never leaves thee, can handle thy daily lot." Jesus put it simpler, yet it has taken nineteen hundred years to arrive at his meaning. "Repent." That is, look back. John the Baptist was mind at one stage of turning toward its pristine starting point. He caught one glad sight of the simplicity of this head center of his own mind and said, *"Behold the lamb of God"*. John 1:35-49)

It is a fact that the wonderful being that, you are at your ever indwelling center is harmless as a lamb, but it is the absolute and eternal God at the same time. It is unburdened, unencumbered innocence, terrible as an army with banners if falsified, healing as balms from the Gilead trees of heaven if spoken truly of, yet doing nothing with mind or body, knowing nothing of either mind or body. For mind and body are the clouds and darkness round about its throne. Talk to it. Tell it the truth of itself so far as you can express. While you are doing this you are forgetting estimations and recognitions. This erases your whole environment forever. You go and dwell nearer your own divinity. The two unnamed men who went and dwelt with Jesus Christ a whole season, namely an evening and a morning, (Verse 39) are the turning back mental tongue and mental eye. The tongue of mind is called "Andrew" when it speaks audibly or writes of Jesus Christ, the pristine "I Am," *"We have found the Christ."*

## The Necessity of Rest

Turning to your own restorative, renewing, inexhaustible reservoir of power, mind, beauty; light, you find that you are rested. This is the rest of God. It is your Jewish Sabbath which is your Gentile Saturday. The Sabbath rest of Jesus Christ is the mighty achievement of humanity. Did you know that there is a divine principle of doing great works by doing nothing? There is. Did you know that you can cure deafness, blindness, conquer poverty, defeat death, renew vitality, by being rested? Look-backward, repent, turn toward the intelligence point, the unquenchable "I Am", at your own center, and talk to it, watch it. When next you have occasion to look around at your environments you will see that many a set of conditions has altered. This is bringing forth the works of repentance. They look like Saturday tasks to the Gentiles, but are known as Sabbath rest to the Jews (or the original people of God).

See what a work John, the repenter, turned off on that Sabbath day here mentioned. These men all represent attitudes of any mind as it first learns of the "I Am," and turns toward it. Nathaniel, the school-bred mind, can hardly believe that an uneducated simpleton, two-thirds knave, can be God. But Philip tells him turn for himself, and that will convince him for the rest.

## The Self-Center No Haltered Joseph

Philip explains that it is the natural outcome of trying to be led around by "impressions," dreams, visions, etc., to finally see that there is a self-center "I" that tells what it wants done and is no haltered "Joseph" but is the dictating "Jesus". (Verse 45)

He who turns toward his own starting point is soon cognizant that he himself foreordained all those experiences he daily has by sending out on the collodions of space half-formed notions. He sees that by so thinking beforehand things that had no truth in them he has predestinated himself to have those dreams, visions, impressions, daily miseries. *"We have found him."*

*"Of whom the law wrote truly,"* (Verse 45) there have been unchanging truths told of the "I Am." But the unalterable glory of its being nigh every one of us, even at our very own center, here awaiting, who has made clear — till now!

*Inter-Ocean Newspaper August 19, 1894*

# LESSON IX

# The First Miracle Of Jesus

*John 2:1-11*

There are two wonderful names of the central spark of divine intelligence in man. Jesus used one of them in his inaugural address on Tel-Hattin, and one of them sixty years after his glorification on the cross. The first is found in the history by Matthew, chapter 5:3, the second in the vision of St. John, chapter 20:1.

The first he realized while fasting in the wilderness of Judea, and second on the while fasting on the Isle of Patmos. The first name is "The Bottomless Pit." It is no wonder that when Pilate asked him the name of God he answered him never a word. For how could he tell aloud that when a mind has dropped thinking about material things at all, and has become so meek to the circumambient spirit that it knows nothing but spirit, it must then let go utterly of even the spirit or it will get as greedy for spirit as it was formerly greedy for material possessions.

How could he say, "The name of the eternal God is The Poor?" *"Blessed are the poor in spirit, for theirs is the kingdom of heaven." The kingdom of heaven is the kingdom of God.* The absolutely poverty-stricken are blessed. They are God. First be meek to spirit and the earth is under your feet. *"Blessed are the meek, for they shall inherit the earth."* Not through wrestling with material things, studying them, counting them, bartering and contriving therewith, but through indifference of them, through interest in spiritual things.

Then, being shorn of spirit, through indifference to spirit, the God who knows no more of spirit than he does of matter, he the already poor in spirit, and the man mind this made devoid, being one mind, this is *"I and the Father are one."* This is God and the spirit is under feet to him.

## "I Myself Am Heaven or Hell"

For thirty years Jesus practiced addressing the divinity spark in his own being, repenting from the ordinary form of language used by his neighbors. He did not claim to have more of the bottomless pit principle, the lake of fire quality, whereby flesh and intellect are swallowed, than other human beings, but he did declare that he turned all the language of his mind toward it, instead of turning it toward descriptions of his bones and sandals, or even toward the education of children in the principles of Phidian sculpture or Socratic logic.

After a certain number of years practice of adoring the self. Jesus discovered what Plato, Gautama, Kwang Tz, and Zoroaster had found out before him, viz., that mankind no matter what sex, or how intelligent, has one common inheritance, a limpid ductile, called mind, which is everlastingly employing a language either silently or audibly, with which it creates heaven or hell, spirit or matter, life or death, foolishness or enlightenment, or neither, at its own dictum:

*"I sent my mind out through the universe,*

*Some letter of the after life to spell.*

*And by and by mind returned to me*

*And answered, "I myself am heaven or hell."*

## The Satan Jesus Recognized

Being meek to spirit he dissolved matter by his molten spiritual quality. Then he saw how he might use his spiritual powers for conquering the Roman phalanxes, for mastering the brilliant Greeks, for owning the gold and precious stones of all the earth, for compelling the minds of a whole globe to fall at his feet in awed astonishment. He declined to exercise such spiritual investment. He let it fall through his open mind, and drop under his feet, fasting there from exactly as he had fasted from employing his mind in thinking of matter.

This was the only Satan such an alert mind could recognize. When he saw that he could manage stones and armies he called that sight of Satan. When he saw how he could govern other minds he called such exercise Satan. It was under the head of "The Temptation" in the August 12 lesson, and may be found in Matt. 4. Not till he had found that the spirit under his feet must blow where it listeth, in entire freedom from the clutch of his mind, was he exalted to such indifference to it that it immediately set every house in order where he appeared without exertion on his part.

Not till he had given the spirit its liberty, through ceasing to hold a mind full of spirit, did he perform the ministry of rest.

## The Rest of the People of God

When you are rested how much you can accomplish without strain. "The rest of the people of God" is when they have ceased to try to be spiritually minded (which is a terribly hard task), and have let the powerful, capable, wise spirit perform according to its own nature, without interference. Does the absolute and eternal "poor" whom we have always with us have to energize and exert his being to bear up the universe? Does the God intelligence have to work himself hard entreating the constellation to wheel aright on their trackless pathways?

*"The poor ye have always with you,"* said Jesus. Did you imagine that the poor that shall forever accompany man, whether he toil as galley slave or speed as archangel, could be the servile women and drugged babies who plead for pennies on our street corners when the matchless science of God has promised that when the *"poor" do take their seats among us, there shall be no more hunger?* Turning backward toward himself Jesus felt the fires of that bottomless abyss of divinity swallowing up death and sorrow in victory. He felt the promise fulfilling itself within himself; *"He will swallow up death in victory."*

His eye being single to it, his body was full of light. He then went forth preaching to all men everywhere to repent, or turn back to watch their own God.

## John the Beholder of Jesus

John the Baptist, who embodied the old dogma of repentance, was beheaded, or rejected; and became John the Beholder of the Jesus Christ in man, as all that is real of man. Last Sunday's lesson taught this in John, first chapter, where the true repentance is beholding the *"Lamb of God that taketh away the sins of the world,"* the divine spark, with its undescribable reserves of intelligence and majesty in all men alike, instead of beholding their outward conducts. Being thus rested from the spirit, Jesus, the free God, would not interfere with the wines at the wedding feast, which is the subject of Today's Bible lesson. (John 2:1-11) He did not take his mother's view of the situation, either as to the lack of wine or his own personal capabilities. She believed that he could manufacture wine out of nothing. He knew that he had nothing to do with wines or personal abilities. *"Woman, what have I to do with thee?"* This is not a disrespectful speech to his mother. Augustus called Cleopatra "woman." Priam, in Homer's Illiad so addresses Hecuba, his Queen. Woman embodies the Holy Spirit principle. Jesus had just come from being poor in spirit. The spiritual woman quality should not reign over him, as the material man quality had long since fallen forgotten beneath him. Poverty of spirit is the unsexed God. This estate of mind gives the spirit freedom to blow its winy winds through waters where wines are asked for, it's healing winds through bodies where health is asked for, it's prospering winds through affairs where prosperity is asked for.

## The Wind of the Spirit

This estate of mind does not make one appear different from his fellow men, or make his speech unusual, except when the moment strikes for unusual speech. *"Bear the wine unto the governor of the feast,"* said the absolutely poor Jesus. With the greedy after spirit there is the lifelong moan," "More! More!" Did any saint ever get chronicled as having spirit enough? With the greedy after gold and silver, the lifelong moan is, "More! More!" Did any Rothschild or Vanderbilt ever be chronicled as having money enough?

But when some repenting mind is swallowed up in his own God all the earth, from governors down to bartenders, shall feel the easy yoke of life more and more. (Verse 9) The struggle to be rich in money now begins to loose its hold on the mind everywhere because the winds of the spirit are let to blow where they list, and they ever list to set the house of man in happy order.

The struggle to be spiritually minded now looses its hold on the awakened in understanding of Jesus Christ. They let the spirit free to blow where it listeth, and it now listeth to blow ambitions and greeds out of all men's minds everywhere.

*Inter-Ocean Newspaper August 26, 1894*

# LESSON X

# Jesus Cleansing the Temple

*John 2:13-25*

Study of the Supreme Principle chemicalizes mind. Thinking over the simple fact that before activity and existence came into being there must have been something preceding them will plunge the subtle essential called mind into a bath of something different from mind. This alters the feelings of mind.

We read of unlearned men being mentally chemicalized by throwing all the energies of their intelligence into contemplation of that Undescribed Fountain from whence they must have drawn their quantum of intelligence, and exhibiting afterward remarkable powers of mind.

The Chinese had a peasant child who thus enlightened his mind! He said: "He who knows others is shrewd, but he only who knows himself is enlightened." He discovered himself by dipping his mind into the origin of himself.

We read of great cowards who made a chemical charge of themselves by employing all of their time in thinking of what was their starting point. They meditated on what Jacob Boehme called the "Mystic Potentiality," the "Abyssal Nothing." They wandered at what Tauler called the "Divine Dark." They forgot everything in Spinoza's "One Substance." They lost time and memory in Kant's "Unconditioned Absolute." They fell unconscious in meditation on Spencer's "Unknowable." The disciples of Jesus are good illustrations. In abject terror "they forsook him and fled," but afterward astonished the governments and armies of their age by their intrepid conduct.

## The Secret of Fearlessness

There is nothing of which that man is afraid whose mind has touched the Absolute. Every motion he makes tells with powerfulness. He makes himself a Jerusalem, or "impregnable position." Thus did the son of Joseph and Mary. At 31 years of age "he made a scourge of small cords and drove" the rich men out of his way, scattered their piled up currency and described himself as one who would raise himself to life again if they should rally strength enough to destroy his body. (John 2:13-25)

When he took notice of the money question at all he advocated hoarding nothing. He taught the direct contact with the Supreme Principle makes mind self-providing. He was not a money maker, through understanding money schemes but through understanding God. He always had money to pay his way with. He easily supplied a large number of purses with gold and silver. He paid all his best friends' taxes. *"Seek ye first the kingdom of God an all these things shall be added unto you."*

Thus we perceive that mind may receive a chemical change whereby it is not terrorized by poverty, but is coolly independent of all things by plunging itself into the origin of itself.

The Chinese peasant who made up his mind to take a different base from which to arrange his life said: "To wear fine clothes and cut a great swath, to eat and drink to satisfy, to lay up superfluous wealth — this I call magnificent robbery." He added: "He who does not know the eternal life wildly works his own misery. He who knows it is magnanimous, broad of spirit, royal; he is heaven itself, yea, the Absolute Principle, the divine Tao, and therefore immortal. Though his body perish he is in no danger." The Chinese peasant's name was Lao-Tzu.

Jerusalem the Symbol of Indestructible Principle

As to the character and effect of the Supreme Principle he discovered the same that Jesus did. Isaiah had discovered the same long before Lao-Tzu spoke in China or Jesus walked in Palestine. Speaking of the mind that has "passed over" the ways and thoughts current among men into the Abyssal Cause, he wrote: *"As the birds flying so will the lord of hosts defend Jerusalem; defending also he will deliver it, and passing over he will preserve it."*

It is not profitable to suppose that this passage meant the city of Jerusalem, for if ever there has lain a God-forsaken ruin it is old Jerusalem. The prophets, the priests, the peasants, who in rapt moments of knowledge of the undescribable Absolute wrote of him wonderful things, used figures of speech. Jerusalem was the symbol of indestructible principle.

Notice that this lesson, meant by its enlightened author to show the majesty of character that the son of the carpenter roused by thirty-one years of constant study of that which was before matter and mind, before worlds and skies, begins by telling of his going up to Jerusalem for the Passover.

The feast of the Passover was in commemoration of the angel of death once passing over their ancient homes. This angel was also the angel of life. He took the Jews into his heart and set them into safety. Jesus had been passed over the doctrines of life and death into an impregnable mountain of independence.

## What is Required of the Teacher

It takes one who has touched the exalted mountains of God's presence, who is not afraid of life or death, to settle the money matters of the nations.

It takes one who has been a peasant in supplies of knowledge and by contact with unearthly wisdom has shown the sages' enlightenment to prove that God is enough for man to know. It takes one who has been a peasant in supplies of money and by contact with unsordid light has shown the millionaire's resources to prove that God is enough for man to know.

In all these ways we have an object lesson and a formula in the story of Jesus. In a partial sense we have the same in the story of Lao-Tzu. Some are contending that he was the equal of Jesus in all ways. You can read his books and judge for yourself.

Their whole theme was: "Be indeed in open daylight what you are in actual fact, the impregnable God himself." "Pass over the stories of your schools. Pass over the methods of your finance. Be Jerusalem, exalted mind."

"For, as the Lord, the Supreme, is entered, the master and the scholar must perish out of the land. The money changers and their banks must feel the crack of doom. When the mind strikes its mainspring it strikes irresistible love. It is chemicalized. Wheresoever it speaks it cracks the mind that hates and its owner disappears. Wheresoever it enters it cracks the mind that hoards and its owner disappears.

## The Whip of Soft Cords

People who are studying the everlasting God that changeth not are very dangerous people to be entering our bank doors. They bring their whip of soft chords. They bring the soft answer that the tellers and cashiers and stockholders cannot hear, but which soundlessly overthrows their whole scheme.

By contact with the irresistible the mind of a serf is God. By practice of touching the exalted presence the mind of a carpenter is Christ Jesus.

Hear ye the tramp of such a host on the slippery streets of closing time? He committed not himself to any man for he already knew all that they knew (Verse 24). He who studies the supreme principle commits not his time to schools. There he would be taught the stupendous dogma that all 'a is x, m is a, therefore m is x'. At the fountain head of wisdom he would find that there is a living Jesus Christ. The living Jesus Christ is in himself. Therefore he is the living Jesus Christ. He commits not himself to the churches. There he would find the glorious doctrine that man's soul is altogether depraved but may surely be saved by believing in the death of God. At the starting point, where the soul was sprung from, he finds that the soul of the murderer is God, and by acquaintance with that soul he manifests God the changeless life. He commits not himself to finance, for there he finds that men are rated by the splendid system of silver circles and gold -weights. At the touch of the Everlasting One that is no respecter of persons he finds that there is but one substance, and in that all share and share alike in free use of the unfailing Father.

He is Jesus Christ.

*"At the Height of his life,*

*I read Love's story,*

*And the key of the world is mine."*

*Inter-Ocean Newspaper, September 2, 1894*

# LESSON XI

# Jesus and Nicodemus

### *John 3:1-16*

A point is position only, without length, breadth or thickness. It holds good in geometry or metaphysics that continuing a point produces a straight line.

Early in practice of metaphysical healing it was custom for certain people to take mental position that, no matter what appearances might argue, every man was an absolutely healthy expression of Divine Health.

This was position only, without length, breadth, or thickness of an external foundation to stand upon. In all cases where the position was maintained steadfastly it lined itself straight forth from its mysterious predicate, and multitudes proved that such a point well continued will expose itself as free, happy health.

If a nation has taken the metaphysical position, regardless of appearances, that all men are born free and equal, it may be logically confident that through the evil and the good of war, famine, pestilence, greed, wealth, material advantage, "equality of mankind" is marching forth from secret heart of serf and king to level them one and all to some basis or other.

On this principle we can see that it would be well for the nation that judicates so presumptuously to define the level upon which it would have its people manifest equality, lest the ditch diggers and pulpit orators get equal in moral deportment or thronely possibilities with the Prince of Wales, or he get to their estate *nolens volens*.(Unwilling or willing)

## Metaphysical Teaching of Jesus

No wonder Plato said "God geometrizes," for whether Plato realized the geometry of metaphysics or not, it is certain that a position maintained secretly or openly by any mind bright or dull, will straightway demonstrate itself.

Jesus of Nazareth was the most wonderful demonstrator of metaphysical propositions that human history records. His positions limned themselves upon the surface of destiny with awe-inspiring speed. To a set of fishy-smelling peasants he said: *"Ye are the light of the world."* Three years from that time they wrote their names on the scrolls of time as suns in whose presence Socrates, Plato, Euripides, and Homer must shine but as candles of speculation.

Today's lesson represents not only historic items, but Christian geometry. (John 2) A member of the Sanhedrin, that stately Jewish body, gathering within its grasp of honor as much note as the United States Senate and Supreme Court combined, came secretly to Jesus and said: "Thou art come from God." Jesus answered him likewise: *"Ye must be born again."* "That is impossible," said the Judge of the Supreme Court. "Easily," answered the metaphysician. Take another predicate, quite different from what you have been holding with respect to the common people, hold it steadily for a right length of time and take notice what a different nation you will make of the Jewish people. Now you are holding them as masses of flesh and blood. That which exposes itself to you must therefore appear with flesh and blood characteristics. Regard them as you have declared I am and they will expose spiritual characteristics.

## Birth-Given Right of Equality

*"That which is born of the flesh is flesh; and that which is born of the spirit is spirit."*

*"It is true that I am of God." "Marvel not that I said ye must be born again."* You surely know

enough of spirit and the action of spirit when it is acknowledged, to admit that nothing will demonstrate so satisfactorily as whatever we affirm of spirit.

"I have heard of abstract reasonings," answered the ruler of the bench, "but I doubt the possibility of the common people, like the men of Theudas, for instance, having groundwork of intelligence to plant a divine postulate in, and expect on this human plane anything like the divine man you are."

"Art thou a judge of the Supreme Bench with the fundamental law that all men are created equal, and knowest not that it will bring thee and thy countrymen into continual upheaval till some equal state if mind, possessions, education, is established? Make the heaven-true point that these and thyself, in common with me, started with equal wisdom, and thou wilt see less and less disposition to avarice and hoarding, less and less dissensions, till the shining wisdom of the living God, is plainly manifest in the speech and conduct of every sentient creature."

Nicodemus, unconvinced, departed. Thus, with the splendid geometry of Jesus plainly stated, for 1,800 years judges and rulers have lived in nonrecognition of their own best powers, and without ever describing to their nations what man by man and community by community might demonstrate of wisdom, majesty, unencumbered life; if singly or in companies they should drop a point on the blackboard of ever present eternity and with eye single to its righteousness bring out the body of shining wisdom prophesied by Jesus, the metaphysician.

## Work of the Heavenly Teacher

"If thine eye be single thy whole body shall be full of light."

From heaven he came. In heaven he dwelt. In heaven he is. They that have slept in the dust since time was the point proposed are feeling the touch of the quickening word that heavenly teacher dropped as a seed into the arable soils of mental ethers, and are stirring to prove his predicate. "God so loved us that he started us all forth from himself with his own everlasting, changeless, undefeatable divinity." (Verse 16)

Whoso lifteth up his voice or pen for the true principles expounded by Christ Jesus shall recognize him as the master school man of the ages for soon he believeth on him as alive forever more, as never having either suffered or died, but only discovering the cross to be the highest signal he could fly from the walls of unbelief, he arose upon it to tell to all ages the story of peace where men cry pain, glory where men cry shame, power where men cry defeat (Verse 14, 15), till the earth shall be filled with the glory of his faithful demonstrations.

*"In the cross of Christ I glory*

    *Towering o'er the wrecks of time,*

*All light of sacred story,*

    *Gathered round its head sublime."*

*Inter-Ocean Newspaper, September 9, 1894*

# LESSON XII

# Jesus at Jacobs Well

*John 4:9-26*

There is a science of influence which may be truly said to rank higher than the science of truth if we judge by history. There are some people who radiate a nameless quality that charms us, cheers us; we love to be where they are; they say no more, they behave no better; they are no kinder, they are no more beautiful, than their companions, but they have liberated from some interior recess a precious ether which comforts the heart.

There is no doubt about every living being having a storage of this same influential ether hidden within him somewhere, but there has been a system of manipulating the apparent being, whether as physical or mental, which has been successful in liberating it except a few formulas handed down the centuries by those whose presence was alive with it; certainly transforming some noninteresting and uninfluential people into more or less strength and charm of character.

All the formulas thus handed down are directly spoken or implied in this lesson of (John 4:26.) And moreover it is here hinted that if any man shall ever arise among us with the genuine science of influence tabulated for instructing us therein so that we certainly may rouse from our secret chambers of being their marvelous reserved resources, that man is the one for whom prophets and sages with their puny speculations, poets and orators with their temporary glimmerings, have waited.

## The Question of the Ages

"We look for such a one," said Socrates. "And when shall he arrive!" asked Alcibiades.

Jesus of Nazareth brought no new truths to mankind. Every truth enunciated had been preached for ages. What then made him touch the Roman army so that it dropped on the ground? What then caused the sun to hide and the rocks to break open? Why, then when his name and character are told to the Brahmins, Buddhists, Shintos. Mohammedans, and Jewish Christians do they begin to slink and shrink, that they may hide or excuse their child widows, sacrifices, and castes? Have they not taught his truths, and in priestly sanctities lived them carefully, age in and age out, from before him in Palestine centuries and centuries, to silence him, ordered off the planet as too powerful to be borne?

It was not the truth he taught, it was not the life he lived, it was not the way he was driven off his globe; it was because he had liberated that interior principle, common to all men, but not in them set free, and knew how to shed it around him, extend it as far, make it as strong, continue it as long, as he pleased.

Why do the moderns practice massage? Because the ancients tried to make themselves believe that kneading and rubbing the body would liberate some of this storage as a healthy aroma from within.

Why do the moderns massage their minds by prayer and formulas? Because the ancients tried to make themselves believe in kneading and rubbing the mind with truths arouse from within some of the living gases, as wisdom, intelligence, understanding, knowledge.

Does massaging the body by pills, quinine, shampooing, or otherwise liberate any of that healing elixir? Does massaging the mind by prayers, memorizings of truths, meditations on aphorisms, axioms, texts, liberate any of that vital elixir of influence in wisdom, judgment, intelligence? How long have these schemes been practiced? Since several thousand years before

Christ. Must there not, then, be something off from genuine in all of them if disease still laughs triumphantly, death has not been defeated, poverty marches independently, ignorance flourishes in the very cities where their most brilliant expounders are holding forth?

## The Great Teacher and Healer

The most successful touch on the springs of mind and body to set free the changeless grandeur stored in all beings was that of Jesus of Nazareth, who admitted that he was the one for whom Socrates had been looking. To the Samaritan he said: *"I that speak unto thee am he."* To her, he said boldly: *"Whosoever shall drink of the water that I will give him shall never thirst."*

She replied by telling with what formulas the Jews had massaged their minds and by what expedients the Samaritans had invigorated their bodies. (Verse 12 and 20)

Suddenly shedding abroad some of the nameless radiance of his interior sunshine, he caused the woman to spring forth as a teacher of men in ways of light. As the sun breaks through cloudy skies and draws up the hidden daisy, so that wonderful influence drew forth the spiritual fervor of the woman at the well.

Ages and generations have come, and gone, but the charm, the warmth, the strength, the wonder of his influence are still as potent as if received on that day. In her time, "as many as touched him were made whole." In our time, as many as attempt to touch him revive in health. In her time, "all who received him to them gave he power to become sons of light." In our time all who receive the influence that is now speeding its hot rays through the parting clouds of time feel something being liberated from within themselves, feel a new life arousing, feel the undefeatable, unconquerable principle springing forth, independent of axiomatic truth, independent of massages of behavior as of sacred nun, or thief on cross; they drink, they live, and the influence of their silent presence is knocking at the gates of all men's minds. They have been the woman at the well in the sense that they have known religious theorems by rote, but in them have found no glory till they knew Jesus Christ.

## "Because I Live Ye Shall Live Also."

The lofty principles with which all Bibles have been for ages filled are cold and slow as the theories of the Hindoos on civilization. The truths that crowd the books on moral philosophy are nerveless and unprompt as Seneca amid the shoals of poverty and riches except they come borne on the wings of influence like his, identical with his, secretly or openly, and indeed because of him, for, *"Because I live ye shall live also."*

He made himself all influence. He unbodied himself. He roused the living principle to his own unformulation, for us to feel the touch thereof, and by it to rise and radiate, not truths, not axioms, not aphorisms, not principles, not examples of rectitude, but unspeakable power. "For the kingdom of God is not in word, but in power." To bring forth our secret chambers of storage the everlasting quality the absolutely unconditioned life entangled not by love of good or hate of vice.

How hard have men worked at massaging their minds with the truth of God, when that which they were striving for was before God was. God is truth. Where did truth come from? Truth is the word that tells how men act when they have felt the Lord's influence. When once a man has tasted of the hidden wells of his own being what does he say? He says: "Do unto others as ye would they should do unto you." How does he act when he has tasted of that influence and roused its like from within himself? He acts out that formula of "Do unto others."

Will conducting himself by that formula give him a taste of his own wells? Will repeating it as an axiom give him a taste? Will receiving the influence that now shines in our midst give him a taste? It will cause him to spring up and be himself what it is, the one of whom if man drink he shall live and his word and life shall be God. He shall know himself.

The perfect word and perfect life are God, but back of the perfect life the perfect word is the Father unconditioned. God is conditioned to goodness, light, mercy, life, health.

## The Faith That Is Needful

He must live and speak truth. But if thou hast faith it must be in that which was before God the truth, thou must have it in the covered wells of thy own being. *"Hast thou faith have it to thyself." "The Father seeketh such to worship him."* (Verse 23)

God is spirit, but the poor in spirit, those that have gone back to the Father that is back of spirit, they tell truth, they live truth, they manifest God. What they say and do is God. But they got their saying and doing, which are God, from being uncovered at the eternal springs of their own native influence. Jesus Christ, thus arising, proclaimed the Father as causing truth and spirit to be manifest.

Had he not said, *"God is spirit?"* Had he not taught that we must be poor in spirit which is poor in God? What can this mean but getting back of truth which is God into the unworded influences that formulate truth as we get back of formulated water into the unformulated influences that set water flowing?

Scholars tell us of the invisible gases that compel visible water. Jesus tells us of the Father, the mighty and undescribed first influence abiding in all men, into whose invisible presence he would resolve himself, to compel God to be manifest in all the earth.

Whoever has wonderful influence independent of personal acquirements has unconsciously or unwittingly received some of the warmth of that here present Father. Whoever understands how to receive the shining influence hither streaming, can never grow less or fail, or die, for what he responds with is his well of unchanging "I am." Whoever thus responds manifests God. Whoever can show all men how to be pristinely natural, how to be themselves, how to strike back to their native influence, that one is Messiah

*Inter-Ocean Newspaper, September 16, 1894*

# LESSON XIII

# Daniel's Abstinence

*Daniel 1:8-20*

It is written that the truth shall make you free, but after you are free you do not need truth any more than you would need a ladder that you had climbed out of Tophet into Paradise by.

Before truth was the Father — the great, unarmed cause. Looking toward the Father for a lifetime produces one of two effects on mind. It makes man speak truth or act divinely. It is oriental to speak truth as a result of keeping your mind's eye on the Absolute One. It is occidental to work miracles of mercifulness as a result of watching the Father.

In our Bible we are taught that when these two results clasp hands we may know that the day of judgment has begun.

They must worship the Father in spirit, which is demonstration, and in truth, which is stillness. *"The Father seeketh such to worship him."* The Bible always tells of pairs of opposites and the effects of their coming to unity. *"Except a man be born of water and spirit." "Born of the word and the life." "Born of spirit and truth."*

When men watch the Father and discover great truths they must get to the spirit of the Father also, or they are not in judgment. It is the everlasting majesty of Jesus of Nazareth that he knew truth and acted spiritually. Had he known truth unwarmed by spiritual love he would have made the core city of Christianity as heartless and merciless as Lhassa, the capital of Buddhism, whence travelers return not to tell the tale of how truth unwarmed by spirit makes men act.

## Knowledge Is Not All

It is noticeable, even in the study of Christian truth, that, except the spirit thereof heat the conduct, its brilliant knowers are as apt to call the human masses cattle as were the mighty adepts when speaking of their unfed, unbefriended Serinagur neighbors. (An area in India territory)

If you know the truth you are not necessarily kind, merciful, considerate, generous. You may feel a stupendous indifference to the sufferings of even your father and mother. You may coldly lash your best friend with unmerited rebukes, or see him defrauded by your indifference to his rights as you opportunely set your wise heel on his neck.

Centuries of truth, absolute truth, have done no better than this for Hindooism. This is one swing of mind as it looks as straight as it can toward the Father. The other swing is the warmth of loving kindness that tells as many lies as it can fabricate about the Father, but feeds the hungry, clothes, the naked, keeps the idea of healing, comforting, teaching, clothing the whole world before itself continually. It really swings as far as it can toward mercifulness and justice. It has for its actual code: "Inasmuch, as ye have done it unto one of the least of these ye have done it unto me."

It has no regard to truth or reason as related to the Great First One. Have we not heard it preached that the Great Father created a Satan to go about as a roaring lion seeking which of us he might devour? This is false. There is no truth in it, but the swing of mind away from truth into deeds causes it to be as untruthful as it pleases and still do wonderful kindnesses.

Gasner told his 3,000 patients that they were possessed with devils. The truth is that there are no devils; there never were but the lie did not hinder his curing his believers of unhappiness, poverty, and tumors.

## Between the Oriental and Occidental Minds

The Christian Scientists tell of the mesmeric wickedness of each other. The truth is that there is no mesmeric wickedness; there could not be, for the good is the only presence, but this fabrication does not hinder their mysterious healing of all manner of disease.

You can tell whether your mind is more Oriental or Occidental in its tendency by noticing whether you ignore demonstrations of goodness and tenderness in your preachings, or urge them as exceedingly vital.

The Jesus Christ mind is the poise between the two, the clasp of their hands, the union of speaking truth and doing good. The day when Oriental truth that cannot be controverted touches the Occidental activity of good is the beginning of the judgment day. As the Father hath committed all judgment unto the Jesus Christ mind, it is Jesus Christ day. The unspeakable glory of the Father is the irresistible influence that is taking the place of both truth and spirit in our very hour.

*"What is this salutes my ear,*

*'Tis Jesus in the atmosphere:*

*'Tis thus the Lord approaches earth,*

*This is the judgment in its birth."*

## The Four Servants of God

Today's lesson brings to our notice four Jewish youths, who were making their struggle to swing from truth into spirit. They had some faint glimpses of the judgment line of dealing with the God who was before truth and spirit, but this lesson of (Daniel 1:8-20), leans hard toward the spirit or the demonstration of good.

They were in a realm where the poor old, deformed, sick, are ignored as our English travelers describe them to this day.

They had come from the land of the Jews, who are to this day noted for their merciful care of the poor, old, sick; the land of Ruth, gleaning in the fields of Boaz, according to their religion of shalt and shalt not: *"When thou cutest down thine harvest in thy field, and has forgot a sheaf in the field, thou shalt not go again to fetch it: it shall be for the stranger, the fatherless, and the widow, that the Lord, thy God may bless thee in all the work of thine hand."* (Deut. 24: 19)

In the land of cold truth, which cast horoscopes and spoke foreign tongues without study of them, but cared nothing for the rights of others, these youths determined to put the activity of good to proof.

## The Saving Power of Good

They had heard one of the commands of the spirit of good given by their own teachers of conduct: *"Prove me now and see if I will not pour you out a blessing."* They told this to the Melzar, or head man in the army of coldness. He answered them: "Then shall ye make one endanger my head." Those who would demonstrate the spirit of truth proposed to save his head. That is truly occidental, for only on that swing are life, health, prosperity, joy precious. The Jews brought the first pull away from truth to the saving power of good. Therefore Jesus taught "Salvation is of the Jews." They fabricated descriptions of God that were not true. They told of his bad temper: "God is angry with the wicked every day." They told of his unreliability: "He will have mercy upon who he will have mercy, and whom he will, he pardoneth."

They told of his cruelty: "And Er, Judah's first born, was wicked in the sight of the Lord, and the Lord slew him." But they felt warmly the certainty that attention to heart to that same being would demonstrate in power of love. They expected health, beauty, strength, prosperity from talking with him. The four Jewish youth are in today's lesson promising the terrified Chaldean wise man that even by eating beans and peas they will fatten. Even by drinking only water they will demonstrate ruddy countenances. And at the end of the days when the King communed with them he found them ten times better than all the magicians and astrologers of truth. (Verses 18, 19, 20)

## The Meeting-Ground of Spirit and Truth

Nothing is directly told in this lesson of the unity day when, because of the occidental mind with its activity of spiritual "works" has touched with the oriental mind that tells absolute truth browbeats good works, the judgment point of mind is felt, which is its free state. But it is esoterically permeated with the information that there is a meeting-ground of earnest spirit and careful truth which shows the face of the highest. At that point it is what we are that sheds its influence on the universe, and not what we say or do.

"Canst thou bind the sweet influences of the Pleiades?" Neither canst thou bind the radiance of the high purposes of the wonderful people who are now in the earth of the same order of mind as the silent three who accompanied the miracle promising Daniel. They preach not, they go not about working miracles, but from their silent fastnesses they close the books of time and the soul of man is free from the thrall of the two religions. That which is not boldly told by this Daniel lesson is what it really means. It means that the soul is master of religion and not religion master of it. It means that when man feels the influence of this fact he is free right where he stands. It means that when he rouses this in himself it is his home. It means that when the soul has thus come home to itself it is the Father, and truly the Father needs no religion.

*Inter-Ocean Newspaper, September 23, 1894*

# REVIEW

*John 2:13-25*

In metaphysics, as in mathematics, it is important that we put two and two together and make four; else we are mystified at the four when it appears. If a traveler in India tells me that the Buddhists are so careful of life that even the life of an animal is sacred to them and then tells me that no white man ever lived to get safely into and out of Lassa, the lore city of Buddhism, I shall instantly compute that the Buddhists strain at gnats and swallow camels like good Christians.

If the traveler in America tells me that the Christians have a God who is too pure to behold iniquity, and yet is angry with the wicked everyday, I shall compute them instantly as slipshod in religion. If he further tells me that the Christians preach that attention to the true God will make them regard not the outward garb of mankind, and then he describes that if one enter into their stately temples who belongs to a gold ring he is forgiven everything he ever did, but if he bear no sign of the gold ring he is forgiven nothing. I shall conclude that they have not paid any attention to the true God, have very little idea of where he keeps himself, and care very little for his opinion of them.

Today's lesson is called the "Review." We are to review the July, August, and September principles, which all religions, both East and West, concur in teaching as mental steps backward toward that intelligence we hailed from.

*"In trailing clouds of glory did we come*

*From God who is our home."*

## Take with You Words.

We are heeding Hosea, who said: "Take with you words and return unto your God." Stepping backwards thus from today we first pause on this golden text of Mark 1:15, and then by the golden texts of each other day we endeavor to remember and remember our way back to our Father's house from whence we all came out.

This golden text is: "The kingdom of God is at hand; repent ye, and believe the gospel."

One cyclopedia, in much use by what are called the common people, tells us that the whole time of the early ministry of the apostles of Christianity was given to establishing the proposition in the mental soil of this globe, that Jesus the Nazarene was the actual presence of God. That he did exactly as God would do manifest as man, that he taught exactly what God meant all men to know, that to keep the mind on him was to keep the mind on God and by him get joyously home again where we all belong.

This cyclopedia tells us that they preached very little of religion of Jesus. Looking them up we find this is greatly true. They called perpetual attention to his name. By this perpetual sound they caused the world to ask what he taught. By learning what he taught they agreed he was wonderful. "They believed on him."

The principle instruction of Jesus was: "The kingdom of God is within you at hand — nigh." He explicitly taught that when a man prays he must pray to his own self. The apostles of Jesus never told me to pray to myself; but Jesus is plain on this point.

## Healing Comes from Within

Gautama of India, had noticed, 400 years before Jesus taught men to pray to themselves, that while he was consecrating himself to cure the world of the four scourges he hated he found that it was forth from some interior region of his own being that he drew the curing power. He sought to rid mankind of disease, poverty, death, old age. He found that there was a God that could do it and that that God was within himself.

Jesus said, "When thou prayest pray to the Father in heaven." Where is heaven? Within you. Who is there in wisdom? God is there. Then when I am repeating, "Our Father," do I mean that the Father that is in me is the same Father as in the low caste Hindu; the Roman Caesar and the Sanhedrin Jew? Yes, one and the same. Does this not divide the God into parts and parcels? Nay, there is no spot or place or where that this same glorious One is not present.

What makes some men seem to me to be so intelligent while others are so dull, if they are equally divine? That is because thou hast not prayed to thyself. Thou knowest not thyself. When thou hast prayed to thyself, thou by that only process knowing thyself first, will know all others next. "Believe this gospel."

The next text before this was, "God gave them knowledge and skill in all learning and wisdom." The cold truth of Brahma, Bel, Osiris, Allah is that man need not labor for his bread for his heavenly Father will take care of his eating. This prompting principle misunderstood makes tramps, fakirs, shiftlessness. But it is the swift melting tenderness of actual gifts straight from the God within and without when the spirit of that truth strikes fire on the mind. It is Jesus -walking everywhere, owning the world.

## The Marthas and Marys of Christianity

It is Martha slamming around crossly, knowing that God will do all the work, but not melted to it enough to sit down, who thinks that if Mary is provided for in idleness it is not fair. It is Mary who is melted to the spirit of the truth that the Lord provides enough to believe that if the president of the republic can be provided for while doing nothing, the unemployed masses have as good a right. But she knows that nobody is safe in his provisions till he sits at the feet of Jesus. That is, understand the God man even within himself. Martha insists, not on all the world's sitting in the sunshine of spirit and truth while universal provisions rain down, but upon nobody's proving the direct loving-kindness of God. She saith: "Bid Mary do as I do."

Daniel and the silent three Jews do thus sit down under the influence of the sunshine of spirit and prove its unspeakable powers.

The disciples of Bel are the Marthas of Christianity. They are determined to mend the world to their enslaving will. The four Jews are the Mary's of Christianity who attempts to bend nobody to their will, but who are representations of what can be done by the Jesus Christ plan. With the rest of the world against their principles practically they softly sway the inner hearts of life, making it a final certainty that it is a God-implanted instinct which causes every creature to choose to have everything and do nothing to earn it. It is the secret of the world's forgiveness of the man born to gold.

When that principle was thus proclaimed by Daniel it secretly stirred the world's life to producing a Jesus who should tell and live it again. And he in his turn is secretly stirring the world mind to producing himself again in all men. When the outward world's of Daniel are preached, men bristle up and oppose them as Melzar, but when their secret influence is felt, as of silent Azariah, Mishall, and Hananiah, lay up for a workless and care-free period in a near future.

## The Summing Up of Golden Texts

Feeling the mystic influence without boldly uttering the truth, they are taking hold of the principle as awkwardly as the tramp. That golden text taught us that it is awkward handling of principles that makes poverty, disease, old age, death, and the secret of man's opposition to them is the great fact that the God within him knows them not and experiences them not.

The other golden texts teach that when all mankind have learned the principal proclamation of Jesus, they are well started toward exhibiting what they have felt the promptings of when struggling to count as worth something somewhere by their native unearned greatness.

That principal proclamation was that the universe is a reproduction to each man of his estimate of himself. If he rates himself as God, the world will be to him full of God. Every movement of it must answer the prayers he prayed to himself.

The sum total of the texts that declare this is enshrined within one as the tooth of Buddha is enshrined within the priceless sapphire. "I am in the Father, and the Father is in me." What estimate hast thou put upon thyself? Thus far that estimate hath determined thy career. A change of estimate will change thy career. Thou hast no destiny only where self-estimation leads.

Jesus taught the stupendous primary that whoever first prays to the Father within himself shall then know his bearings on this strange journey we are all taking. Till he does this, he does nothing that counts.

*Inter-Ocean Newspaper, September 30, 1894*

# Notes

# Other Books by Emma Curtis Hopkins

- *Class Lessons of 1888 (WiseWoman Press)*
- *Bible Interpretations (WiseWoman Press)*
- *Esoteric Philosophy in Spiritual Science (WiseWoman Press)*
- *Genesis Series*
- *High Mysticism (WiseWoman Press)*
- *Self Treatments with Radiant I Am (WiseWoman Press)*
- *Gospel Series (WiseWoman Press)*
- *Judgment Series in Spiritual Science (WiseWoman Press)*
- *Drops of Gold (WiseWoman Press)*
- *Resume (WiseWoman Press)*
- *Scientific Christian Mental Practice (DeVorss)*

## Books about Emma Curtis Hopkins and her teachings

- *Emma Curtis Hopkins, Forgotten Founder of New Thought* – Gail Harley
- *Unveiling Your Hidden Power: Emma Curtis Hopkins' Metaphysics for the 21st Century (also as a Workbook and as A Guide for Teachers)* – Ruth L. Miller
- *Power to Heal: Easy reading biography for all ages* –Ruth Miller

To find more of Emma's work, including some previously unpublished material, log on to:

www.highwatch.org
www.emmacurtishopkins.com

800. 603.3005

# WISEWOMAN PRESS

## Books Published by WiseWoman Press

### By Emma Curtis Hopkins

- *Resume*
- *Gospel Series*
- *Class Lessons of 1888*
- *Self Treatments including Radiant I Am*
- *High Mysticism*
- *Esoteric Philosophy in Spiritual Science*
- *Drops of Gold Journal*
- *Judgment Series*
- *Bible Interpretations: series I, thru XIV*

### By Ruth L. Miller

- *Unveiling Your Hidden Power: Emma Curtis Hopkins' Metaphysics for the 21st Century*
- *Coming into Freedom: Emily Cady's Lessons in Truth for the 21st Century*
- *150 Years of Healing: The Founders and Science of New Thought*
- *Power Beyond Magic: Ernest Holmes Biography*
- *Power to Heal: Emma Curtis Hopkins Biography*
- *The Power of Unity: Charles Fillmore Biography*
- *Power of Thought: Phineas P. Quimby Biography*
- *Gracie's Adventures with God*
- *Uncommon Prayer*
- *Spiritual Success*
- *Finding the Path*

Watch our website for release dates and order

www.wisewomanpress.com

# List of Bible Interpretation Series with date from 1st to 14th Series.

This list is complete through the fourteenth Series. Emma produced about thirty Series of Bible Interpretations.

She followed the Bible Passages provided by the International Committee of Clerics who produced the Bible Quotations for each year's use in churches all over the world.

Emma used these for her column of Bible Interpretations in both the Christian Science Magazine, at her Seminary and in the Chicago Inter-Ocean Newspaper.

## First Series

### July 5 - September 27, 1891

| | | |
|---|---|---|
| Lesson 1 | The Word Made Flesh<br>*John 1:1-18* | July 5th |
| Lesson 2 | Christ's First Disciples<br>John 1:29-42 | July 12th |
| Lesson 3 | All Is Divine Order<br>*John 2:1-1*1 (Christ's first Miracle) | July 19th |
| Lesson 4 | Jesus Christ and Nicodemus<br>*John 3:1-17* | July 26th |
| Lesson 5 | Christ at Samaria<br>*John 4:5-26* (Christ at Jacob's Well) | August 2nd |
| Lesson 6 | Self-condemnation<br>*John 5:17-30* (Christ's Authority) | August 9th |
| Lesson 7 | Feeding the Starving<br>*John 6:1-14* (The Five Thousand Fed) | August 16th |
| Lesson 8 | The Bread of Life<br>*John 6:26-40* (Christ the Bread of Life) | August 23rd |
| Lesson 9 | The Chief Thought<br>*John 7:31-34* (Christ at the Feast) | August 30th |
| Lesson 10 | Continue the Work<br>*John 8:31-47* | September 6th |
| Lesson 11 | Inheritance of Sin<br>*John 9:1-11, 35-38* (Christ and the Blind Man) | September 13th |
| Lesson 12 | The Real Kingdom<br>*John 10:1-16* (Christ the Good Shepherd) | September 20th |
| Lesson 13 | In Retrospection | September 27th<br>Review |

## Second Series

### October 4 - December 27, 1891

| | | |
|---|---|---|
| Lesson 1 | Mary and Martha<br>*John 11:21-44* | October 4th |
| Lesson 2 | Glory of Christ<br>*John 12:20-36* | October 11th |
| Lesson 3 | Good in Sacrifice<br>*John 13:1-17* | October 18th |
| Lesson 4 | Power of the Mind<br>*John 14:13; 15-27* | October 25th |
| Lesson 5 | Vines and Branches<br>*John 15:1-16* | November 1st |
| Lesson 6 | Your Idea of God<br>*John 16:1-15* | November 8th |
| Lesson 7 | Magic of His Name<br>*John 17:1-19* | November 15th |
| Lesson 8 | Jesus and Judas<br>*John 18:1-13* | November 22nd |
| Lesson 9 | Scourge of Tongues<br>*John 19:1-16* | November 29th |
| Lesson 10 | Simplicity of Faith<br>*John 19:17-30* | December 6th |
| Lesson 11 | Christ is All in All<br>*John 20: 1-18* | December 13th |
| Lesson 12 | Risen With Christ<br>*John 21:1-14* | December 20th |
| Lesson 13 | The Spirit is Able<br>Review of Year | December 27th |

# Third Series

## January 3 - March 27, 1892

| | | |
|---|---|---|
| Lesson 1 | A Golden Promise<br>*Isaiah 11:1-10* | January 3rd |
| Lesson 2 | The Twelve Gates<br>*Isaiah 26:1-10* | January 10th |
| Lesson 3 | Who Are Drunkards<br>*Isaiah 28:1-13* | January 17th |
| Lesson 4 | Awake Thou That Sleepest<br>*Isaiah 37:1-21* | January 24th |
| Lesson 5 | The Healing Light<br>*Isaiah 53:1-21* | January 31st |
| Lesson 6 | True Ideal of God<br>*Isaiah 55:1-13* | February 7th |
| Lesson 7 | Heaven Around Us<br>*Jeremiah 31 14-37* | February 14th |
| Lesson 8 | But One Substance<br>*Jeremiah 36:19-31* | February 21st |
| Lesson 9 | Justice of Jehovah<br>*Jeremiah 37:11-21* | February 28th |
| Lesson 10 | God and Man Are One<br>*Jeremiah 39:1-10* | March 6th |
| Lesson 11 | Spiritual Ideas<br>*Ezekiel 4:9, 36:25-38* | March 13th |
| Lesson 12 | All Flesh is Grass<br>*Isaiah 40:1-10* | March 20th |
| Lesson 13 | The Old and New Contrasted<br>Review | March 27th |

# Fourth Series

## April 3 - June 26, 1892

| | | |
|---|---|---|
| Lesson 1 | Realm of Thought<br>*Psalm 1:1-6* | April 3rd |
| Lesson 2 | The Power of Faith<br>*Psalm 2:1-12* | April 10th |
| Lesson 3 | Let the Spirit Work<br>*Psalm 19:1-14* | April 17th |
| Lesson 4 | Christ is Dominion<br>*Psalm 23:1-6* | April 24th |
| Lesson 5 | External or Mystic<br>*Psalm 51:1-13* | May 1st |
| Lesson 6 | Value of Early Beliefs<br>*Psalm 72: 1-9* | May 8th |
| Lesson 7 | Truth Makes Free<br>*Psalm 84:1-12* | May 15th |
| Lesson 8 | False Ideas of God<br>*Psalm 103:1-22* | May 22nd |
| Lesson 9 | But Men Must Work<br>*Daniel 1:8-21* | May 29th |
| Lesson 10 | Artificial Helps<br>*Daniel 2:36-49* | June 5th |
| Lesson 11 | Dwelling in Perfect Life<br>*Daniel 3:13-25* | June 12th |
| Lesson 12 | Which Streak Shall Rule<br>*Daniel 6:16-28* | June 19th |
| Lesson 13 | See Things as They Are<br>Review of 12 Lessons | June 26th |

# *Fifth Series*

## July 3 - September 18, 1892

| | | |
|---|---|---|
| Lesson 1 | The Measure of a Master<br>*Acts 1:1-12* | July 3rd |
| Lesson 2 | Chief Ideas Rule People<br>*Acts 2:1-12* | July 10th |
| Lesson 3 | New Ideas About Healing<br>*Acts 2:37-47* | July 17th |
| Lesson 4 | Heaven a State of Mind<br>*Acts 3:1-16* | July 24th |
| Lesson 5 | About Mesmeric Powers<br>*Acts 4:1-18* | July 31st |
| Lesson 6 | Points in the Mosaic Law<br>*Acts 4:19-31* | August 7th |
| Lesson 7 | Napoleon's Ambition<br>*Acts 5:1-11* | August 14th |
| Lesson 8 | A River Within the Heart<br>*Acts 5:25-41* | August 21st |
| Lesson 9 | The Answering of Prayer<br>Acts 7: 54-60 - Acts 8: 1-4 | August 28th |
| Lesson 10 | Words Spoken by the Mind<br>*Acts 8:5-35* | September 4th |
| Lesson 11 | Just What It Teaches Us<br>*Acts 8:26-40* | September 11th |
| Lesson 12 | The Healing Principle<br>Review | September 18th |

# Sixth Series

## September 25 - December 18, 1892

| | | |
|---|---|---|
| Lesson 1 | The Science of Christ<br>*1 Corinthians 11:23-34* | September 25th |
| Lesson 2 | On the Healing of Saul<br>*Acts 9:1-31* | October 2nd |
| Lesson 3 | The Power of the Mind Explained<br>*Acts 9:32-43* | October 9th |
| Lesson 4 | Faith in Good to Come<br>*Acts 10:1-20* | October 16th |
| Lesson 5 | Emerson's Great Task<br>*Acts 10:30-48* | October 23rd |
| Lesson 6 | The Teaching of Freedom<br>*Acts 11:19-30* | October 30th |
| Lesson 7 | Seek and Ye Shall Find<br>*Acts 12:1-17* | November 6th |
| Lesson 8 | The Ministry of the Holy Mother<br>*Acts 13:1-13* | November 13th |
| Lesson 9 | The Power of Lofty Ideas<br>*Acts 13:26-43* | November 20th |
| Lesson 10 | Sure Recipe for Old Age<br>*Acts 13:44-52, 14:1-7* | November 27th |
| Lesson 11 | The Healing Principle<br>*Acts 14:8-22* | December 4th |
| Lesson 12 | Washington's Vision<br>*Acts 15:12-29* | December 11th |
| Lesson 13 | Review of the Quarter | December 18th |
| Partial Lesson | Shepherds and the Star | December 25th |

## *Seventh Series*

### January 1 - March 31, 1893

| | | |
|---|---|---|
| Lesson 1 | All is as Allah Wills | January 1st |
| | *Ezra 1* | |
| | Khaled Knew that he was of The Genii | |
| | The Coming of Jesus | |
| Lesson 2 | Zerubbabel's High Ideal | January 8th |
| | *Ezra 2:8-13* | |
| | Fulfillments of Prophecies | |
| | Followers of the Light | |
| | Doctrine of Spinoza | |
| Lesson 3 | Divine Rays Of Power | January 15th |
| | *Ezra 4* | |
| | The Twelve Lessons of Science | |
| Lesson 4 | Visions Of Zechariah | January 22nd |
| | *Zechariah 3* | |
| | Subconscious Belief in Evil | |
| | Jewish Ideas of Deity | |
| | Fruits of Mistakes | |
| Lesson 5 | Aristotle's Metaphysician | January 27th |
| | Missing (See Review for summary) | |
| Lesson 6 | The Building of the Temple | February 3rd |
| | Missing (See Review for summary) | |
| Lesson 7 | Pericles and his Work in building the Temple | |
| | *Nehemiah 13* | February 12th |
| | Supreme Goodness | |
| | On and Upward | |
| Lesson 8 | Ancient Religions | February 19th |
| | *Nehemiah 1* | |
| | The Chinese | |
| | The Holy Spirit | |
| Lesson 9 | Understanding is Strength Part 1 | February 26th |
| | *Nehemiah 13* | |
| Lesson 10 | Understanding is Strength Part 2 | March 3rd |
| | *Nehemiah 13* | |
| Lesson 11 | Way of the Spirit | March 10th |
| | *Esther* | |
| Lesson 12 | Speaking of Right Things | March 17th |
| | *Proverbs 23:15-23* | |
| Lesson 13 | Review | March 24th |

# *Eighth Series*

### April 2 - June 25, 1893

| | | |
|---|---|---|
| Lesson 1 | The Resurrection | April 2nd |
| | *Matthew 28:1-10* | |
| | One Indestructible | |
| | Life In Eternal Abundance | |
| | The Resurrection | |
| | Shakes Nature Herself | |
| | Gospel to the Poor | |
| Lesson 2 | Universal Energy | April 9th |
| | *Book of Job, Part 1* | |
| Lesson 3 | Strength From Confidence | April 16th |
| | *Book of Job, Part II* | |
| Lesson 4 | The New Doctrine Brought Out | April 23rd |
| | *Book of Job, Part III* | |
| Lesson 5 | The Golden Text | April 30th |
| | *Proverbs 1:20-23* | |
| | Personification Of Wisdom | |
| | Wisdom Never Hurts | |
| | The "Two" Theory | |
| | All is Spirit | |
| Lesson 6 | The Law of Understanding | May 7th |
| | *Proverbs 3* | |
| | Shadows of Ideas | |
| | The Sixth Proposition | |
| | What Wisdom Promises | |
| | Clutch On Material Things | |
| | The Tree of Life | |
| | Prolonging Illuminated Moments | |
| Lesson 7 | Self-Esteem | May 14th |
| | *Proverbs 12:1-15* | |
| | Solomon on Self-Esteem | |
| | The Magnetism of Passing Events | |
| | Nothing Established by Wickedness | |
| | Strength of a Vitalized Mind | |
| | Concerning the "Perverse Heart" | |

| | | |
|---|---|---|
| Lesson 8 | Physical vs. Spiritual Power | May 21st |

*Proverbs 23:29-35*
Law of Life to Elevate the Good and Banish the Bad
Lesson Against Intemperance
Good Must Increase
To Know Goodness Is Life
The Angel of God's Presence

| | | |
|---|---|---|
| Lesson 9 | Lesson missing | May 28th |

(See Review for concept)

| | | |
|---|---|---|
| Lesson 10 | Recognizing Our Spiritual Nature | June 4th |

*Proverbs 31:10-31*
Was Called Emanuel
The covenant of Peace
The Ways of the Divine
Union With the Divine
Miracles Will Be Wrought

| | | |
|---|---|---|
| Lesson 11 | Intuition | June 11th |

*Ezekiel 8:2-3*
*Ezekiel 9:3-6, 11*
Interpretation of the Prophet
Ezekiel's Vision
Dreams and Their Cause
Israel and Judah
Intuition the Head
Our Limited Perspective

| | | |
|---|---|---|
| Lesson 12 | The Book of Malachi | June 18th |

*Malachi*
The Power of Faith
The Exercise of thankfulness
Her Faith Self-Sufficient
Burned with the Fires of Truth
What is Reality
One Open Road

| | | |
|---|---|---|
| Lesson 13 | Review of the Quarter | June 25th |

*Proverbs 31:10-31*

# Ninth Series

## July 2 - September 27, 1893

| | | |
|---|---|---|
| Lesson 1 | Secret of all Power | July 2nd |
| Acts 16: 6-15 | The Ancient Chinese Doctrine of Taoism | |
| | Manifesting of God Powers | |
| | Paul, Timothy, and Silas | |
| | Is Fulfilling as Prophecy | |
| | The Inner Prompting. | |
| | Good Taoist Never Depressed | |
| Lesson 2 | The Flame of Spiritual Verity | July 9th |
| Acts 16:18 | Cause of Contention | |
| | Delusive Doctrines | |
| | Paul's History | |
| | Keynotes | |
| | Doctrine Not New | |
| Lesson 3 | Healing Energy Gifts | July 16th |
| Acts 18:19-21 | How Paul Healed | |
| | To Work Miracles | |
| | Paul Worked in Fear | |
| | Shakespeare's Idea of Loss | |
| | Endurance the Sign of Power | |
| Lesson 4 | Be Still My Soul | July 23rd |
| Acts 17:16-24 | Seeing Is Believing | |
| | Paul Stood Alone | |
| | Lessons for the Athenians | |
| | All Under His Power | |
| | Freedom of Spirit | |
| Lesson 5 | (Missing) Acts 18:1-11 | July 30th |
| Lesson 6 | Missing No Lesson * | August 6th |
| Lesson 7 | The Comforter is the Holy Ghost | August 13th |
| Acts 20 | Requisite for an Orator | |
| | What is a Myth | |
| | Two Important Points | |
| | Truth of the Gospel | |
| | Kingdom of the Spirit | |
| | Do Not Believe in Weakness | |

| | | |
|---|---|---|
| Lesson 8 | Conscious of a Lofty Purpose | August 20th |
| *Acts 21* | As a Son of God | |
| | Wherein Paul failed | |
| | Must Give Up the Idea | |
| | Associated with Publicans | |
| | Rights of the Spirit | |
| Lesson 9 | Measure of Understanding | August 27th |
| *Acts 24:19-32* | Lesser of Two Evils | |
| | A Conciliating Spirit | |
| | A Dream of Uplifting | |
| | The Highest Endeavor | |
| | Paul at Caesarea | |
| | Preparatory Symbols | |
| | Evidence of Christianity | |
| Lesson 10 | The Angels of Paul | September 3rd |
| *Acts 23:25-26* | Paul's Source of Inspiration | |
| | Should Not Be Miserable | |
| | Better to Prevent than Cure | |
| | Mysteries of Providence | |
| Lesson 11 | The Hope of Israel | September 10th |
| *Acts 28:20-31* | Immunity for Disciples | |
| | Hiding Inferiorities | |
| | Pure Principle | |
| Lesson 12 | Joy in the Holy Ghost | September 17th |
| *Romans 14* | Temperance | |
| | The Ideal Doctrine | |
| | Tells a Different Story | |
| | Hospitals as Evidence | |
| | Should Trust in the Savior | |
| Lesson 13 | Review | September 24th |
| *Acts 26-19-32* | The Leveling Doctrine | |
| | Boldness of Command | |
| | Secret of Inheritance | |
| | Power in a Name | |

# Tenth Series

## October 1 – December 24, 1893

| | | |
|---|---|---|
| Lesson 1 | *Romans 1:1-19* | October 1st |
| | When the Truth is Known | |
| | Faith in God | |
| | The Faithful Man is Strong | |
| | Glory of the Pure Motive | |
| Lesson 2 | *Romans 3:19-26* | October 8th |
| | Free Grace. | |
| | On the Gloomy Side | |
| | Daniel and Elisha | |
| | Power from Obedience | |
| | Fidelity to His Name | |
| | He Is God | |
| Lesson 3 | *Romans 5* | October 15th |
| | The Healing Principle | |
| | Knows No Defeat. | |
| | In Glorified Realms | |
| | He Will Come | |
| Lesson 4 | *Romans 12:1* | October 22nd |
| | Would Become Free | |
| | Man's Co-operation | |
| | Be Not Overcome | |
| | Sacrifice No Burden | |
| | Knows the Future | |
| Lesson 5 | *I Corinthians 8:1-13* | October 29th |
| | The Estate of Man | |
| | Nothing In Self | |
| | What Paul Believed | |
| | Doctrine of Kurozumi | |
| Lesson 6 | *I Corinthians 12:1-26* | November 5th |
| | Science of The Christ Principle | |
| | Dead from the Beginning | |
| | St. Paul's Great Mission | |
| | What The Spark Becomes | |
| | Chris, All There Is of Man | |
| | Divinity Manifest in Man | |
| | Christ Principle Omnipotent | |

| | | |
|---|---|---|
| Lesson 7 | *II Corinthians 8:1-12* <br> Which Shall It Be? <br> The Spirit is Sufficient <br> Working of the Holy Ghost | November 12th |
| Lesson 8 | *Ephesians 4:20-32* <br> A Source of Comfort <br> What Causes Difference of Vision <br> Nothing But Free Will | November 19th |
| Lesson 9 | *Colossians 3:12-25* <br> Divine in the Beginning <br> Blessings of Contentment <br> Free and Untrammeled Energy | November 26th |
| Lesson 10 | *James 1* <br> The Highest Doctrine <br> A Mantle of Darkness <br> The Counsel of God <br> Blessed Beyond Speaking | December 3rd |
| Lesson 11 | *I Peter 1* <br> Message to the Elect <br> Not of the World's Good | December 10th |
| Lesson 12 | *Revelation 1:9* <br> Self-Glorification <br> The All-Powerful Name <br> Message to the Seven Churches <br> The Voice of the Spirit | December 17th |
| Lesson 13 | Golden Text <br> Responding Principle Lives <br> Principle Not Hidebound <br> They Were Not Free Minded | December 24th |
| Lesson 14 | Review <br> It is Never Too Late <br> The Just Live by Faith <br> An Eternal Offer <br> Freedom of Christian Science | December 31st |

# *Eleventh Series*

## January 1 – March 25, 1894

| | | |
|---|---|---|
| Lesson 1 | *Genesis 1:26-31 & 2:1-3* | January 7th |
| | The First Adam | |
| | Man: The Image of Language Paul and Elymas | |
| Lesson 2 | *Genesis 3:1-15* | January 14th |
| | Adam's Sin and God's Grace | |
| | The Fable of the Garden | |
| | Looked-for Sympathy | |
| | The True Doctrine | |
| Lesson 3 | *Genesis 4:3-13* | January 21st |
| | Types of the Race | |
| | God in the Murderer | |
| | God Nature Unalterable | |
| Lesson 4 | *Genesis 9:8-17* | January 28th |
| | God's Covenant With Noah | |
| | Value of Instantaneous Action | |
| | The Lesson of the Rainbow | |
| Lesson 5 | I Corinthians 8:1-13 | February 4th |
| | *Genesis 12:1-9* | |
| | Beginning of the Hebrew Nation | |
| | No Use For Other Themes | |
| | Influence of Noble Themes | |
| | Danger In Looking Back | |
| Lesson 6 | *Genesis 17:1-9* | February 11th |
| | God's Covenant With Abram | |
| | As Little Children | |
| | God and Mammon | |
| | Being Honest With Self | |
| Lesson 7 | *Genesis 18:22-23* | February 18th |
| | God's Judgment of Sodom | |
| | No Right Nor Wrong In Truth | |
| | Misery Shall Cease | |
| Lesson 8 | *Genesis 22:1-13* | February 25th |
| | Trial of Abraham's Faith | |
| | Light Comes With Preaching | |
| | You Can Be Happy NOW | |

| | | |
|---|---|---|
| Lesson 9 | *Genesis 25:27-34* | March 4th |
| | Selling the Birthright | |
| | "Ye shall be Filled" | |
| | The Delusion Destroyed | |
| Lesson 10 | *Genesis 28:10-22* | March 11th |
| | Jacob at Bethel | |
| | Many Who Act Like Jacob | |
| | How to Seek Inspiration | |
| | Christ, the True Pulpit Orator | |
| | The Priceless Knowledge of God | |
| Lesson 11 | *Proverbs 20:1-7* | March 18th |
| | Temperance | |
| | Only One Lord | |
| | What King Alcohol Does | |
| | Stupefying Ideas | |
| Lesson 12 | *Mark 16:1-8* | March 25th |
| | Review and Easter | |
| | Words of Spirit and Life | |
| | Facing the Supreme | |
| | Erasure of the Law | |
| | Need No Other Friend | |

# Twelfth Series

## April 1 – June 24, 1894

| | | |
|---|---|---|
| Lesson 1 | *Genesis 24:30, 32:09-12*<br>Jacob's Prevailing Prayer<br>God Transcends Idea<br>All To Become Spiritual<br>Ideas Opposed to Each Other | April 8th |
| Lesson 2 | *Genesis 37:1-11*<br>Discord in Jacob's Family<br>Setting Aside Limitations<br>On the Side of Truth | April 1st |
| Lesson 3 | *Genesis 37:23-36*<br>Joseph Sold into Egypt<br>Influence on the Mind<br>Of Spiritual Origin | April 15th |
| Lesson 4 | *Genesis 41:38-48*<br>Object Lesson Presented in<br>the Book of Genesis | April 22nd |
| Lesson 5 | *Genesis 45:1-15*<br>"With Thee is Fullness of Joy"<br>India Favors Philosophic Thought<br>What These Figures Impart<br>The Errors of Governments | April 29th |
| Lesson 6 | *Genesis 50:14-26*<br>Changes of Heart<br>The Number Fourteen<br>Divine Magicians | May 6th |
| Lesson 7 | *Exodus 1:1-14*<br>Principle of Opposites<br>Power of Sentiment<br>Opposition Must Enlarge | May 13th |
| Lesson 8 | *Exodus 2:1-10*<br>How New Fires Are Enkindled<br>Truth Is Restless<br>Man Started from God | May 20th |
| Lesson 9 | *Exodus 3:10-20*<br>What Science Proves<br>What Today's Lesson Teaches<br>The Safety of Moses | May 27th |

| | | |
|---|---|---|
| Lesson 10 | *Exodus 12:1-14* <br> The Exodus a Valuable Force <br> What the Unblemished Lamp Typifies <br> Sacrifice Always Costly | June 3rd |
| Lesson 11 | *Exodus 14:19-29* <br> Aristides and Luther Contrasted <br> The Error of the Egyptians <br> The Christian Life not Easy <br> The True Light Explained | June 10th |
| Lesson 12 | *Proverbs 23:29-35* <br> Heaven and Christ will Help <br> The Woes of the Drunkard <br> The Fight Still Continues <br> The Society of Friends | June 17th |
| Lesson 13 | *Proverbs 23:29-35* <br> Review <br> Where is Man's Dominion <br> Wrestling of Jacob <br> When the Man is Seen | June 24th |

# *Thirteenth Series*

## July 1 – September 30, 1894

| | | |
|---|---|---|
| Lesson 1 | The Birth of Jesus | July 1st |
| | *Luke 2:1-16* | |
| | No Room for Jesus | |
| | Man's Mystic Center | |
| | They glorify their Performances | |
| Lesson 2 | Presentation in the Temple | July 8th |
| | *Luke 2:25-38* | |
| | A Light for Every Man | |
| | All Things Are Revealed | |
| | The Coming Power | |
| | Like the Noonday Sun | |
| Lesson 3 | Visit of the Wise Men | July 15th |
| | *Matthew 1:2-12* | |
| | The Law Our Teacher | |
| | Take neither Scrip nor Purse | |
| | The Star in the East | |
| | The Influence of Truth | |
| Lesson 4 | Flight Into Egypt | July 22nd |
| | *Mathew 2:13-23* | |
| | The Magic Word of Wage Earning | |
| | How Knowledge Affect the Times | |
| | The Awakening of the Common People | |
| Lesson 5 | The Youth of Jesus | July 29th |
| | *Luke2:40-52* | |
| | Your Righteousness is as filthy Rags | |
| | Whatsoever Ye Search, that will Ye Find | |
| | The starting Point of All Men | |
| | Equal Division, the Lesson Taught by Jesus | |
| | The True Heart Never Falters | |
| Lesson 6 | The "All is God" Doctrine | August 5th |
| | *Luke 2:40-52* | |
| | Three Designated Stages of Spiritual Science | |
| | Christ Alone Gives Freedom | |
| | The Great Leaders of Strikes | |
| Lesson 7 | Missing | August 12th |
| Lesson 8 | First Disciples of Jesus | August 19th |
| | *John 1:36-49* | |
| | The Meaning of Repentance | |

|  |  |  |
|---|---|---|
| | Erase the Instructed Mind | |
| | The Necessity of Rest | |
| | The Self-Center No Haltered Joseph | |
| Lesson 9 | The First Miracle of Jesus | August 26th |
| | *John 2:1-11* | |
| | "I Myself am Heaven or Hell" | |
| | The Satan Jesus Recognized | |
| | The Rest of the People of God | |
| | John the Beholder of Jesus | |
| | The Wind of the Spirit | |
| Lesson 10 | Jesus Cleansing the Temple | September 2nd |
| | *John 2:13-25* | |
| | The Secret of Fearlessness | |
| | Jerusalem the Symbol of Indestructible Principle | |
| | What is Required of the Teacher | |
| | The Whip of Soft Cords | |
| Lesson 11 | Jesus and Nicodemus | September 9th |
| | *John 3:1-16* | |
| | Metaphysical Teaching of Jesus | |
| | Birth-Given Right of Equality | |
| | Work of the Heavenly Teacher | |
| Lesson 12 | Jesus at Jacob's Well | September 16th |
| | *John 4:9-26* | |
| | The Question of the Ages | |
| | The Great Teacher and Healer | |
| | "Because I Live, Ye shall Live Also." | |
| | The Faith That is Needful | |
| Lesson 13 | Daniel's Abstinence | September 23rd |
| | *Daniel 1:8-20* | |
| | Knowledge is Not All | |
| | Between the Oriental and Occidental Minds | |
| | The Four Servants of God | |
| | The Saving Power of Good | |
| | The Meeting-Ground of Spirit and Truth | |
| Lesson 14 | Take With You Words | September 30th |
| | *John 2:13-25* | |
| Review | Healing Comes from Within | |
| | The Marthas and Marys of Christianity | |
| | The Summing up of The Golden Texts | |

# Fourteenth Series

## October 7 – December 30, 1894

| | | |
|---|---|---|
| Lesson 1 | Jesus At Nazareth | October 7th |
| *Luke 4:16-30* | Jesus Teaches Uprightness | |
| | The Pompous Claim of a Teacher | |
| | The Supreme One No Respecter of Persons | |
| | The Great Awakening | |
| | The Glory of God Will Come Back | |
| Lesson 2 | The Draught of Fishes | October 14th |
| *Luke 5:1-11* | The Protestant Within Every Man | |
| | The Cry of Those Who Suffer | |
| | Where the Living Christ is Found | |
| Lesson 3 | The Sabbath in Capernaum | October 21st |
| *Mark 1:21-34* | Why Martyrdom Has Been a Possibility | |
| | The Truth Inculcated in Today's Lesson | |
| | The Injustice of Vicarious Suffering | |
| | The Promise of Good Held in the Future | |
| Lesson 4 | The Paralytic Healed | October 28th |
| *Mark 2:1-12* | System Of Religions and Philosophy | |
| | The Principle Of Equalization | |
| | The Little Rift In School Methods | |
| | What Self-Knowledge Will Bring | |
| | The Meaning Of The Story of Capernaum | |
| Lesson 5 | Reading of Sacred Books | November 4th |
| *Mark 2:23-38* | The Interior Qualities | |
| *Mark 2:1-4* | The Indwelling God | |
| | Weakness Of The Flesh | |
| | The Unfound Spring | |
| Lesson 6 | Spiritual Executiveness | November 11th |
| *Mark 3:6-19* | The Teaching Of The Soul | |
| | The Executive Powers Of The Mind | |
| | Vanity Of Discrimination | |
| | Truth Cannot Be Bought Off | |
| | And Christ Was Still | |
| | The Same Effects For Right And Wrong | |
| | The Unrecognized Splendor Of The Soul | |

| | | |
|---|---|---|
| Lesson 7 | Twelve Powers Of The Soul | November 18th |
| *Luke 6:20-31* | The Divine Ego in Every One | |
| | Spiritual Better than Material Wealth | |
| | The Fallacy Of Rebuke | |
| | Andrew, The Unchanging One | |
| Lesson 8 | Things Not Understood Attributed to Satan | |
| *Mark 3:22-35* | True Meaning Of Hatha Yoga | November 25th |
| | The Superhuman Power Within Man | |
| | The Problem of Living and Prospering | |
| | Suffering Not Ordained for Good | |
| | The Lamb in the Midst shall Lead | |
| Lesson 9 | Independence of Mind | December 2nd |
| *Luke 7:24-35* | He that Knoweth Himself Is Enlightened | |
| | The Universal Passion for Saving Souls | |
| | Strength From knowledge of Self | |
| | Effect Of Mentally Directed Blows | |
| Lesson 10 | The Gift of Untaught wisdom | December 9th |
| *Luke 8:4-15* | The Secret Of Good Comradeship | |
| | The Knower That Stands in Everyone | |
| | Laying Down the Symbols | |
| | Intellect The Devil Which Misleads | |
| | Interpretation Of The Day's Lesson | |
| Lesson 11 | The Divine Eye Within | December 16th |
| *Matthew 5:5-16* | Knowledge Which Prevails Over Civilization | |
| | The Message Heard By Matthew | |
| | The Note Which shatters Walls Of Flesh | |
| Lesson 12 | Unto Us a Child I s Born | December 23rd |
| *Luke 7:24-35* | The Light That is Within | |
| | Significance Of The Vision of Isaiah | |
| | Signs of the Times | |
| | The New Born Story Of God | |
| | Immaculate Vision Impossible To None | |
| Lesson 13 | Review | December 30th |
| *Isaiah 9:2-7* | That Which Will Be Found In The Kingdom | |
| | Situation Of Time And Religion Reviewed | |
| | Plea That Judgment May Be Righteous | |
| | The Souls Of All One And Changeless | |

Made in the USA
Charleston, SC
25 May 2012